Afterlife Spirit

M000119342

Preparing for a Positive Passing Into the Afterlife

Overcoming Fears of Dying & Death

Wordstreams, Vignettes, and Reflections

By

Mark Jay Mann

Published by:

Breakthrough Enterprises
P.O. Box 5511
Eugene, OR 97405

Editing, formatting, and cover design by Doug Hoss
(Doug Hoss Media Productions)

ISBN: 978-0-9828990-1-4

Dedicated to the memories of those who have transitioned into the afterlife...

...and to those remaining in the earth realm who have summoned the spiritual courage to prepare for their eventual transitioning into the afterlife.

Acknowledgements

I want to express a special acknowledgement and appreciation to Doug Hoss of Doug Hoss Media Productions for editing and formatting the Kindle and print editions. Besides the essential contributions of his amazing skills, his friendship was instrumental in enabling a flowing creative process that allowed me to complete this book.

I want to express an appreciation to Susan Astle Paradis for her detailed proofreading and her thoughtful and encouraging feedback.

I want to express appreciation to my family, who has provided me sustaining love and support for my writing efforts. And to Diana Zelaya, my love partner, whose transformative sharing while living, and then after passing in 2018 ultimately allowed me to connect more fully with the spiritual wonders of the afterlife.

Table of Contents

Introduction — How Many of You Have Thought About Dying, Death and the Afterlife?

I t's not my intent to put you on the spot...or to make you feel uncomfortable if you haven't explored or made peace with inevitability of you dying.

So I'll share first — then I encourage you to feel if it's important to choose to reflect and determine how you might want to prepare for your eventual dying, death and entering into whatever comes next. I know more and more people have begun to expand their spiritual awareness and acceptance of their own death, but our society still has a death phobia that keeps many from exploring, not just the pain and loss, but also the wonderment of entering into a new dimension of being.

So again, it's not my intent to make you feel uncomfortable if you haven't made peace with the inevitability of your own death, though feeling uncomfortable can be the first phase of people making transformative changes in their lives.

I confess it was not until I was 73 years old and the love of my life for 41 years died that I realized I wanted to understand dying and death and the afterlife more fully...MORE FULLY? What did that mean for me? To not just think of dying and death as some distant event, an event I did not want to think about, not even fear because I only let the actuality of death dwell in my thoughts for brief seconds before I focused my attention on what I was doing...what I wanted to do — TO LIVE LIFE MORE FULLY...

After my love partner died...and then during the following year, after other close friends and my young grandson died, I started to contemplate the question of how might I be able to understand dying and death more fully. Eventually I realized that I was phrasing the question in the wrong way. I began asking myself more directly, *how do I understand my OWN dying and death and what the afterlife might be for me?*

Once I put this question in such personal terms, I began to understand I would be required to not just think about it, but to experience what my dying, death and entering into the afterlife would be like — experience it with my whole being, allowing my psyche to imagine what I would experience as I died — to imagine dying physically, emotionally and spiritually.

Physically, what pain would I be experiencing? Would I have to endure lingering levels of pain, and medications to relieve the pain? What would the side effects of these medications be like for my psyche, my cognitive abilities, and energy levels? Would I be able to think clearly? Would I be able see clearly? Would I be able to communicate with my loved ones? Would I be able to read or watch TV or hold a phone to text or see a photograph that one of my children or grandchildren posted on Instagram? Would I be able to walk, go to the toilet by myself or would I have to have caregivers?

Or would I die suddenly with little pain, but not being able to say goodbye to those I care about? What would it be like to die suddenly, not with a lingering illness? What would it be like to have a car hit me head-on killing me instantly without providing me any opportunity to contemplate whether or not I would survive the crash? What would it be like to die by falling down stairs in a freak accident, or having someone walk up to me on the street and shoot me in the head...or...oh my, so many unforeseen possibilities of dying...?

Emotionally, if I knew I would be dying soon from an illness, what fears, joys, regrets, hopes, and feelings of loss of connections to my loved ones would I be feeling...the loss of my vibrancy, the loss of achieving my goals...the loss of experiencing the satisfactions of my accomplishments...the loss of going out to sit in a café...the loss of walking out in nature...the loss of being able to continue to look directly into the eyes of my loved ones and connect and share emotionally?

Spiritually, would I have developed connections to beyond life dimensions...connections within and beyond myself allowing me to draw on the wisdom of knowing that where I am transitioning to will be joyful, comforting, nurturing, multi-dimensional, liberating, beyond liberating, and/or healing? Would I have gained an understanding of non-rational, transcendental levels of being...and beyond understanding, would I have been able to experience these dimensions through various rituals of spiritual receptivity? Would I have been able to allow myself to explore and delve into areas of consciousness and spiritual being that I had not explored before...that might initially be disorienting and fearing?

This book is an expression of my thoughts, reflections, vignettes, poetic expressions, and understandings as I have, and am, continuing to progress through my personal journey to enter into and understand the dimensions of dying, death and the afterlife while I am alive...not just with my abstract mind, but with opening my psyche to allow my consciousness to connect experientially with the transcendental and spiritual beyond life dimensions.

This book reflects my process of opening myself to and accessing the transpersonal and transcendental faculties that I have long before recognized exists within my psyche — and all of our psyches, to help me transition in peace when my time to die comes, and to live more fully in each moment before I die.

This book is not a "how-to" book, nor is it structured with chapters or a narrative arc. It is a collection of vignettes, my reflections, prose poems and Wily Wizard's humorous, wise guidance. The structure of the book does loosely follow the following arc of thought: the fears of dying and death, visions of the afterlife, transcending the fear of dying and death, and various ways of establishing connections with beyond life dimensions that will assist in preparing for a positive passing into the afterlife.

Many of the wordstreams and vignettes are fictional, although my beyond life guide, **Wily Wizard,** wants me to emphasize that he is real, as real as can be when an essence exists in different dimensions. I can at least attest to my belief that evolved and caring nonsense and humor can help us all transcend our fears.

I had a difficult time coming up with a title for this book based on using the word, *death,* in the title. I eventually realized that the dilemma I was experiencing was symbolic of the theme of this book...how do we transcend our fears of death and dying and the unknowns related to the afterlife? I then wrote about my process of determining an appropriate title (See Appendix II).

I know that many individuals will come to their own understandings of what dying, death and the afterlife means to them. There are many books and media now exploring this transformative event that will come at the end of our lives on this earth.

My own journey continues, of course, even though I feel fortunate that I have been able to identify rituals, concepts, and beliefs that are meaningful to me, and have given me peace and joy as I continue to express my spark of being — while at the same time I am developing a relationship with beyond life dimensions, including the afterlife — that are positive and interactive while I am still living in this earth realm without fear.

Hopefully sharing some of my journey through my writings will stimulate your own journeys to become aware of and deepen your own comforting connection to beyond life dimensions and to your own eventual transition into the wonderment of the afterlife.

As She Was Dying From Alzheimer's

She lay on her bed not knowing who she was or who was caring for her. He had just come into the room, and somehow, she knew his name...unconnected to anything she could remember...but she felt comfort and care in his presence...

Above her she kept envisioning the light, a stream of light that seemed to be inviting her to come into a different place...a place that seemed warm and beautiful...she smiled when she saw the light and almost felt herself leaving to follow its happiness...she had forgotten that she was in her body, that she could not physically move any longer, but she knew that she could travel to the source of the stream of light. Somehow she knew she was not limited to where she lay just because she had forgotten how to move her body...she didn't even know she had forgotten, or that she was even limited by her body...she just knew she was drawn to following the stream of light to somewhere that would give her a peace of spirit and would allow her to dance again...she envisioned herself dancing away as she streamed into the golden light...though she had even forgotten that she had forgotten how to dance...somehow looking into the stream of golden light she remembered...

Then she looked at the man who had come into the room, and who seemed to be caring and comforting her...and she felt a connection to him as warm and loving as the golden stream of light beckoning her...then she felt his touch as he straightened her blanket and he helped to position her more comfortably in her bed, and she watched as he leaned over her, and she felt his lips as he kissed her cheek...

Suddenly she felt confused about what she should be doing...should she drift into the golden stream of light or remain where she was with this man whom she felt was a part of her...connected to her. She wondered how she could leave someone whom was such a loving part of her and she felt confused about leaving him behind.

She heard him say something but could not understand his words...yet she felt a release, a rush of joy, and she somehow remembered a time she had healed a bird with a broken wing, and then was able to release it to fly away...she remembered spreading her hands as she released the bird into the sky...and then knew that something different was happening to her...not only was she feeling released, she remembered something...and she was beginning to realize that remembering meant she was being healed...she became more aware of who she had been, who this man was who seemed to have the capacity to help her enter into the healing golden light, and she remembered that she was a mother, and she remembered who her children and grandchildren are, and as she found herself feeling an expansive sense of joy knowing that she now remembered, she remembered everything...all her experiences in her life and all she will experience.

As she remembered her past life on earth and envisioned what lay before her, she felt a joy knowing she would still be connected with all whom she loved in the life she would be leaving, and she knew she would be visiting them often.

As she drifted away into the golden thread of the afterlife, she felt she was dancing again...

When I Die — Waterfalls of Love

I want to enter the afterlife sliding down a gently sloping waterfall rock incline with exhilarating, rushing rapids smoothing my slide into a pool of refreshing water, where I will transform into the most beautiful golden fish.

I will swim my soul to the other bank, where I will rise out of the water in a formless essence of being as I float above and beyond the earth...in search of you, my love. When I find you, I imagine we will again be able to blend together and enjoy all of the passionately spiritual love we always used to share with each other.

When I Die — A Field of Wildflowers

I hope to find myself in a field of wildflowers...meadowsweet white bulbs swaying in the winds of the afterlife, pale pink musk mallow with sweet scents beyond earthly fragrances, purple loosestrife petals, red clover colors of joy...

...with butterflies dancing underneath what are possibly skies, bees buzzing around (I'm allergic to bees, but I guess it doesn't matter if I'm dead — but OMG we don't know if allergies exist in the afterlife — I'm sure that won't matter...)

I imagine I will be lying on my back in this warm and peaceful field, without allergies, surrounded by lovely and fragrant wildflowers...

I imagine I will be gazing up at the blue sky — well, hopefully there will be a sky, maybe some kind of star that provides one of the lights of life and the afterlife. Maybe I'll become a star and will meld with other stars? Maybe I'll have the spiritual powers to create and become the expansive and comforting blue sky...

Crossing the Ocean

I imagine that when I die, the essence of my soul will float within a boat made of the bones of my body, intertwined with wood from branches of the tree of my life experiences.

I imagine that a lovely variety of flowers will adorn this small boat, the petals of white lotuses taken from spiritual waters, blending with the sweet fragrance of daffodils...

...flowers from the gardens I have cultivated and grown with my hands sensually reaching into the nurturing earth, spreading, and caressing the soil as I planted the seeds of my future potentials...

...flowers that continue to be born, die and be reborn through season after season of my life, with their multi-colored petals unfolding among the vibrant, dark green leaves that have received the vibrant light of the sun, allowing my potentials to bloom.

I imagine that when I die the essence of my soul will float within in a boat adorned with the dried blossoms from the wild flowers representing the joys and sufferings, the accomplishments and disappointments, potentials actualized, purposes achieved in this life, and efforts made to overcome my imbalances, even if I was not always successful.

I imagine that when I die the essence of my soul will float within a boat held together with the natural glue of wisdom from the knowledge that the experiences of my life allowed me to develop; wisdom based on the caring for all living beings and other forms; then the search for spiritual understandings from belief systems that are both inclusive and expansive — this wisdom I believe will hold the boat together until it dissolves into the distant seas floating into other dimensions.

I imagine that when I die, my family and friends, and perhaps a stranger or two, will gently but firmly push me out onto the waves of the ocean, the new beginnings of my spirit journey that will lead me into other dimensions not existing on maps within the oceans of this world... and as my boat containing the essence of my soul glides across the surfaces of the waves of this reality, I will become a sea spirit...

I imagine being surrounded by welcoming essences from beyond life dimensions as I am transcending away the shores of earth's natural environment into the caressing and magical waters of the ocean of the afterlife...

Discussions of a Family and Friends Around a Dinner Table About Death and the Afterlife

A little over a year earlier Celeste had died of cancer at the age of 51. Her husband, Brian, age 55, and their two children (Jeremy-18 and Emily-16) were visiting and having dinner with long-time close family friends (Laura and Ron, who were also in their late 50s).

Celeste and Brian had been together for 26 years before she had passed. Their son, Jeremy was tall for his age, and had just graduated from high school. Emily had dark curly hair like her mom, and her hazel eyes and aura seemed to convey an ethereal quality for those who knew her.

Laura and Ron lived in a small two-bedroom near a forest just outside the city limits. The interior of their house was designed warmly with paintings and fabric art from around the world, and a light wood book case with a variety of books, many about gardening and alternative healing, as well as fiction by mostly European writers. The kitchen was in the same room as the dining table, and after Laura and Ron brought the food to the table, they sat down to enjoy their dinner.

Brian sat at one end of the wooden square table across from his friend, Ron. Laura sat by Emily across from Celeste's son, Jeremy. Laura and Ron had fixed soup and salad and a chicken casserole. Also on the table was a bottle of Cabernet wine and natural soft drinks for the kids.

After a bit of light small talk and pleasantries, Brian said that since Celeste had passed, he felt the urge to explore death and dying and the afterlife.

He said, "Celeste and I had never spent a lot of time talking about the issue of death and dying. We did generally believe in reincarnation. Celeste had studied Sufism when she was in her twenties after she left Catholicism. She had read parts of the Tibetan Book of the Dead and other books exploring various aspects of spirituality. But we had never talked about what the afterlife meant to us very much. It's been meaningful to me to begin to review and explore what I do know about different religious views of the afterlife, but also to explore different ideas such as the shamanic, pagan and various metaphysical ideas of what the afterlife may be. I am very open to exploring this, not only as a way of connecting again with Celeste, but also as a way to prepare for my own passing. And then I have been surprised at how satisfying, even enjoyable, it is for me to imagine various possibilities of what the afterlife might be."

Brian's friend, Ron, who had been listening to him intently, shook his head and responded, "I don't know, I don't want to spend my time thinking about something I can never know for sure until after I die, even if I know anything then. There may be nothing in afterlife. We can't know. I would rather think of the good memories we've had with Celeste and not dwell on something we can't know."

Brian said, "I am choosing to do both, and I do believe that there are enough indications that there is an afterlife — perhaps the existence of many different dimensions. Besides, there are many things in life and beyond that the rational mind cannot measure and see. So often science discovers some aspects of life that previously have not been seen or measured because of limited instruments. We have to be open. At least I feel drawn to opening myself to afterlife possibilities for my own preparation for dying, not just because I want to stay connected with Celeste — even though that is definitely a deep and powerful motivation for me."

Ron took a sip of his wine, and then bending his head to one side and squinting a bit said, "Brian, I can understand what you are saying. But I have to admit, death and dying are not things we should worry about or dwell on. Why dwell on death and dying and the afterlife? Sure, we all have to face this when our loved ones pass and when we are about to pass, but let's focus on living life to the fullest while we are living. Let's focus on things that we can see and hear and are somewhat in control of when we are alive."

Laura then entered the conversation, "But Ron, I understand what Brian is saying. You can do both, if you are so inclined. I think that when someone close to you dies — a love partner, a child, a parent, or a close friend, it does force you to consider the realms of the afterlife."

Brian said, "I am beginning to believe that if our society encouraged everyone — even the young and younger adults — to reflect on spiritual realities related to death and dying, it would be healthier — there would not be so much fear around death. And many spiritual teachers and psychologists believe that it would actually help people to embrace life more fully and to take advantage of each moment of life." Ron nodded his head, but his expression indicated he was not convinced.

Then Brian looked at Laura, and continued, "You know, some spiritual teachers say that it is better to just let a loved one who has passed go to allow them to embrace their new journeys in the afterlife, instead of trying to keep them hanging around this reality. This is something I've struggled with because I realize that trying to stay connected to someone you've loved and lost could be selfish. But for me, Celeste's death has allowed me to become more open to spiritual realities. I've always imagined and believed in the existence of alternate realities, though I've never been inclined to develop sides of myself that would allow me to perhaps connect with these realities, except with my imagination. Now I do want to see if I can connect with these other realities through conscious efforts, through rituals and discipline."

Brian stopped talking and looked at Jeremy and Emily who seemed to be listening to the discussion intently. They were normally used to hanging out with older adults, and even joining into discussions but Brian became concerned that this discussion about their mother's death might not be so comfortable for his kids.

Laura picked up on Brian's concern about how Jeremy and Emily might feel about this discussion. She said, "I wonder if this is this something we should not be talking about right now. Jeremy...Emily...let's catch up on what you two have been doing."

But Jeremy said, "Laura, it's ok. We've had discussions like this from time to time since Mom died. Sure, during some of these discussions, it's been difficult, and at times I haven't wanted to talk about it, even think about my mom dying and death and the afterlife. But I've realized it's been helpful. Actually, before mom died, she talked openly with us about her passing, and tried to prepare us that everything would be ok, and that while she would miss us, she wanted us to help her move on to her next journey. It was difficult at first for me to accept this."

He stopped talking as he began to tear up. Laura reached over and put her hand on his hand. Jeremy eventually continued, "You know, my mom always cried so easily. I also cry easily, and when I was younger it bothered me so much. I tried to control it. Mom always told me when she cried that her tears were often expressions of feelings of joy overflowing from her heart and soul and at other times tears of sadness. She said she hoped I would be comfortable with crying in special moments. She said tears gave her joy as much as helped her release her sadness. As I grew older, she helped me become comfortable with crying. Now I feel my mom is soothing me when I cry."

He stopped for a moment as he continued to compose himself. Then he looked at his Dad, and continued. "I am aware of your interest in exploring the afterlife since you sometimes share what you're reading and thinking about. I'm not sure where I am on this. I haven't felt like reading about death and dying and what the afterlife is about before now. But I guess because my mom has died, I have been more aware of death and dying, and have thought about the afterlife more. I just hope that wherever mom is she's peaceful...and happy." He looked at Ron before continuing, "I do feel good when Dad shares with me some of his thinking..." but then he smiled as he looked back at his Dad, and added, "Most of the time."

Brian smiled back at this son, and responded, "Of course, you can always tell me if I am talking too much...and I may listen..."

Emily had been listening closely to this discussion. She had felt a wave of sadness come over her at the beginning of this talk about the death of her mom. But the waves of sadness quickly receded, and she actually felt thankful listening to how everyone was expressing their love and sometimes lightness, despite their feelings of loss.

Emily knew that her mom was probably around her still — she would see her mom at night before she went to sleep and often felt her kissing her goodnight. Emily remembered fondly her mom telling her that she was her psychic child — that she had special psychic abilities. As Emily grew older, she realized she saw and felt things that other people didn't, and she became thankful that her mom and Dad had encouraged her to develop this ability, while also providing guidance in how to balance these perceptions with objective reasoning and remaining grounded in this world — in the here and now.

Emily finally said, "I'm also ok Laura...and Dad, talking about mom's passing...you know, I feel connected with mom in the afterlife. I miss her so much, but I still see and feel her all the time in my dreams and throughout the day. I know she's around me and it feels comforting."

Brian smiled at his daughter and leaned over and hugged her. He often felt comforted by seeing how much Jeremy and Emily had qualities of his wife, their mother.

Everyone had finished dinner. Ron clapped his hands and said, "OK, how about a game? Something like..." He stopped talking as he looked at Jeremy and Emily, but after a moment continued, "OK, I can see on your faces that you kids are not game for a game..." He laughed and Jeremy and Emily rolled their eyes, but laughed also. Ron suggested, "OK, how about a walk in the woods — it's still light out, or a movie."

Emily spoke, "How about a walk in the woods, and then maybe a movie...or a game if you really want to."

Brian said, "Let's do it!" and they all got up to clean up before going for their walk.

Celeste, who had been listening to their conversations, let the following thoughts and feelings flow through her consciousness: "What a wonder family I have...had! Well, both, I guess."

When she first had passed, she had been surprised and felt gratified that she was able to perceive reality on the other side of life as she had known it, and in which she had existed. She had been surprised that she remained conscious of herself and who she had been in her recent life. She was somehow watching her husband, her children and her friends talking about her and the afterlife. She felt a sense of satisfaction when Jeremy talked about being OK with crying, even around others, and when Emily described that she often felt her presence. Since she had passed, she had continued to kiss her daughter goodnight, and also her husband and son...but she didn't know how long she would be able to do this. She somehow knew she had to leave soon on her new journey. But in her new existence she wondered if she could be in many places at the same moment? She thought...what do moments even mean in her current being? She sensed that there were many other places, if that is what she could call where she was and was going, places and dimensions she was meant to explore...and many other beings to connect with, blend with. She wondered if she would always be able to remember who she was and her loved ones in the life she had just left. She hoped that would be the case. She somehow felt that a part of her consciousness would always remain with her family and close friends, along with understandings and qualities she had developed in this recent past life. She hoped that she could eventually convey to her loved ones that she was at peace and even more that she was excited about her new journeys in her new incarnations.

She wanted to release their sense of sadness. But listening to her children and her husband during this dinner gathering, and also at other times before, she already knew they would be ok, and would be embracing life while remembering the best parts of her.

She knew she would be leaving soon, but she felt she would be returning from time to time to kiss them goodnight, and then would be able to greet them when each entered this lovely new afterlife.

As she watched them begin their walk, she decided she would stay with them for a little while through their walk in the forest before she floated away again.

Wily Wizard Discusses Death and the Afterlife

Wily Wizard from beyond life dimensions likes to visit the earth and other physical realms to give his nonsensical, esoteric guidance to those who appreciate good spiritual laughs and jokes.

Somehow, he found himself agreeing to do an interview with a host of a local digital streaming talk show while he was in one of his disguises as a shaman (which he often chose since shamans are one of the human beings in the earth realm closely connected to beyond life dimensions in the earth realm).

Interviewer: Thank you for agreeing to come into our online stream to discuss death and the afterlife.

Wily Wizard: You call this a stream? It's more like drip, an infinitesimally small drop in infinitely diverse dimensions...

(Interviewer looks confused)

Wily Wizard: Sorry...sometimes it's not easy to confine myself to drips and drops...this or that. It's what you call it that makes it so unreal.

Interviewer: I'm not sure what you mean?

Wily Wizard: Sorry... How about asking me a specific question or a ridiculous question? I enjoy the ridiculous as much as...anyway do you have a question?

Interviewer: Can you enlighten us about what occurs when a human dies?

Wily Wizard: Mostly, it's the cessation of breathing air in the earth realm.

Interviewer: Is that all? Is that all you can say about death? What do you believe happens after a person dies?

Wily Wizard: Well, there are many different aspects to dying — sometimes it's like leaving a role as a clown in a carnival to become an opera singer — or vice versus, depending on...well, many things and choices an individual might have made or might want to make.

Interviewer (slowly shaking his head): I don't understand what on earth you are talking about.

Wily Wizard: That's because we are talking about matters and existences that transcend our lives on earth. By the way, would you rather be a clown or an opera singer? You don't have to answer that really because there are many other dimensions of being that we can choose from than those two. And I think I already know what you answer would be anyway.

Writer's revision notes:

Make it more nonsensical or a little more sensual — no I mean sensical — no, no — I mean sensible. Sensational?

Maybe I need to revise it to make it more of all of these ways of non-being.

Or is this wily wizard trying to distract and confuse me rather than guide me as I try to write about this spiritually obtuse interview?

Healthy Skepticism and Spiritual Openness About the Afterlife

A friend recently asked me if I could explain my view of the afterlife. When I shared some of my thoughts, he then shared his thoughts. He said that he believed most people's view of the afterlife was based on fear, and that people tended to latch onto a belief system they were exposed to by religion or a spiritual teacher to develop their ideas about the afterlife to make themselves feel better and to relieve their fears.

I shared that the process of dying can be spiritually enhanced by developing an awareness of what the afterlife is. Gaining an awareness of what the afterlife is requires a holistic blend of non-rational, transcendental receptivity, as well as a reasonable dose of rational objectivity. It requires a blend of skepticism, which does involve the rational mind, and yet also requires a transcendental openness which allows the psyche to enter into transcendental dimensions.

We are all capable of entering into these beyond life dimensions while we are living in the earth ream. It takes a willingness to go on a journey into the spiritual unknown.

It also takes a willingness to seek guidance from others who have attained connections with spiritual dimensions. How do we know if our perceptions and those of spiritual guides and teachers are accurate? We have to be willing to trust in our capacities to know what is real by continuing to use this blend of intuition and rationality.

We have to be willing to rise above a rigidly extreme skepticism. As historian Richard Tarnas, wrote in his book, <u>Cosmos and Psyche</u>:

"Only with discernment and inward opening can the full participatory engagement unfold that brings forth new realities and new knowledge.

Without the capacity, at once active and receptive, the long discipline would be fruitless.

The carefully cultivated skeptical posture would become finally an empty prison, an armored state of unfulfillment, a permanently confining end in itself rather than the rigorous means to a sublime result."

We also have to be willing to rise above dogma that attempt to control others. We have to be willing to be wrong, and yet trust in what seems a common experience of spiritual transformation.

It takes both a spiritual desire and effort; both a healthy skepticism blended with spiritual openness.

When I Die — If Nothing Else Exists...

...I won't know anyway, right?

S o while I'm alive I will continue to imagine what I want the afterlife to be. I will continue to imagine the afterlife consists of exquisite multiple spiritual dimensions where all essences of beings who have transitioned exist with their unique consciousness intact in evolved states.

I will continue to imagine these spiritual potentials are not just fantasies that keep me from addressing realities of life and death...

When I die, I want to imagine that spiritual dimensions do exist. But if nothing really exists, I have enjoyed my spiritual fantasies (even though I will never believe they are just fantasies unless I'm proven wrong...but how will I know if nothing exists after I die? Hmmm.)

I will continue to enjoy, be comforted and inspired by my visions of the afterlife...and if you allow yourself to also become attuned to and envision beyond life dimensions, these spiritual inner connections will enhance your life and allow you to overcome your fears of dying.

When I Die — My Unique Consciousness Will Continue

W hen I die, I believe I will keep my unique consciousness. I will know who I am...or was... the essence of whom I have always been and will be, even as I continue to evolve, not in a hierarchal manner, but in a spiritually holistic manner, not rising to some higher level, but expanding out in all directions incorporating more of who I can be, as I connect and interact lovingly with all other essences of being.

I will continue to be...as I AM...Am I too selfish to think this? I do not believe so...I choose to believe that I'm — and all of us — are essences of uniqueness continuing when we die — as we have grown through the time-space seasonal phases and cycles within earth realms and other physical realms...and then when we die, we will continue to evolve our uniqueness in dimensions beyond the seasons.

The Statistics of Birth and Death

How many births have occurred since the beginning of recorded history? How many deaths?

According to the Population Reference Bureau in Washington, there have been about 107 billion people who have been born and lived, but that there are currently 7 billion people alive today. According to these estimates, there are 15 dead people for every person living. Apparently, we passed the 7 billion people dead between 8000 BCE and the first years of the Common Era!

It appears to be unimaginable, then, that there will ever be more alive than dead people who have been born. This would mean that Earth would have to have the capacity of sustain 100–150 billion people.

In 2015, worldwide, there were about 140 million births and 57 million deaths. Yet there are predictions that births will decrease and deaths increase and become about equal by the end of the century. In the US in 2017 there were 3.86 million births and 2.81 million deaths.

According to provisional data from the National Center for Health Statistics (NCHS) National vital Statistics System (NVSS) the leading causes of causes of deaths in the US in 2020 were:

- Heart disease: 690,882
- Cancer: 598,932
- COVID-19: 345,223
- Accidents (unintentional injuries): 192,176
- Stroke (cerebrovascular diseases): 159,050
- Chronic lower respiratory diseases: 151,637
- Alzheimer's disease: 133,382
- Diabetes: 101,106
- Influenza and pneumonia: 53,495
- Kidney disease: 52,260
- Intentional self-harm (suicide): 44,831

Total deaths: 3,358,814 — an increase in deaths of 503,967 (17.7%) from 2,854,838 in 2019.

As of June 15, 2021, according to Worldmeter, the number of deaths that have occurred in the US from the COVID-19 reached 600,000.

Besides the political and population ramifications of these statistics in the US, these numbers reflect a growing need to address the medical and general caregiving related to those dying as well as the psychological-spiritual processes of preparing to die without trauma or fear. Otherwise, these statistics become meaningless.

A Woman Dies Not Knowing What Happened...

...until she became aware of her essence of being in the afterlife.

It was an aneurysm. She wondered why it happened so suddenly. She was only 25-years-old, and she had always been so healthy.

But as she experienced her essence of being in the afterlife, her questions of why it happened began to fade away...she began feeling the sense of spiritual awe, comfort and excitement...as other essences of being flowed near her, welcomed her and embraced her.

Then she thought about her family, her lover, her friends, her career, her dreams of what she wanted to accomplish in her life on earth...but she did not feel sorrow. Oh, she knew she would miss her recent life, but she had the awareness that she had done what she could do in the best way she could while she was living in her body on earth. She knew that now she had other spiritual journeys to make to not only develop her own essence of being more fully, but to also contribute to the well-being of all existence in ways that she could, and feeling this purpose gave her joy...

But what about the loved ones she was no longer able to share experiences with? Ah, she became aware that humans are not limited just to their rational minds, and the ones who develop their transcendental emotional and mental faculties will still be able to share with her and others in beyond life dimensions while they are still living.

She felt a new sense of excitement and joy as she recognized another spiritual purpose for herself...to find ways of encouraging and helping those still living to develop the capacities to see essences of being like her and to share in fulfilling ways beyond the limits of time and space of the earth realm. She would look for guidance and spiritual mentoring from other essences of being.

And just then an essence of being floated up to her and introduced himself as Wily Wizard. She was surprised that she felt like laughing with feelings of comedy and anticipation in his presence even though she didn't know who he was.

"Let me tell you an afterlife joke," he said. She giggled and said she somehow already knew the punch line...

"You are the joke, Wily Wizard, that we have to take with a grain of salt as we traverse these nonsensical afterlife dimensions..."

Wily Wizard thanked her and complimented her on adding that bit about the salt which he said doesn't make any sense in these dimensions, and then they both floated away laughing.

During the Decades of Life: Are We Helping Each Other to Prepare for a Good Death and to Transcend Our Fear of Dying?

O f course, the decades of our lives do not make us who we become and are when we die — it's the choices that are made for us while we are children, or that we make as we become an adult during these significant and common phases of life that make us who we are. Our choices, made consciously or not, determine our abilities to actualize in positive ways our unique potentials as we mature through the decades of our lives. Our choices to explore and define our spiritual beliefs, especially related to dying and death, determine if we are preparing for a positive passing.

The 1st Decade of Life

The first decade after birth, we are just meant to be a baby becoming a child...to let our faculties and bodies grow and develop. We are guided to learn how to care and respect others in social situations, even as we are enjoying the spontaneity of the spark of life building into a fire of consciousness as we learn to talk, read, take care of our bodies, think, and express emotions. Some individuals may have past life memories that often tend to fade away before we learn to talk, but can be accessed later in life through consciously expanding hypnotic and shamanic techniques.
But, in this first decade of life, how come many of our parents or mentors never talk about or expose us to the dying and death and the existences beyond life dimensions — in positive ways that can prepare us to transcend the fear of dying?

The 2nd Decade of Life

During the second decade of life, things become more complex as our hormones burst forward, blossoming with desires as we learn how to balance assertiveness with receptivity, in ways that encourage sensitivity to others, yet in ways that do not put out our positive fires and feelings of our being; in ways that help us develop a secure feeling of self-love and acceptance; in ways that help us learn to limit our selfishness so that we do not become narcissistic or abusive.

But how come during this decade so few of us are exposed to the existences beyond life — to death and the afterlife — in positive ways that can enhance both the young person to transcend the fear of dying?

The 3rd Decade of Life

In our twenties we are meant to explore and experiment in determining our unique purposes and interests, to find suitable and satisfying career directions — and to continue to learn how to express our own desires within an interdependence union of a romantic love partner — all as we develop our individual maturity as the decade comes to a transition.

But, during this decade, how many of us are encouraged and/or choose to explore spiritual existences beyond life in an open, non-rigidly skeptic manner — and to embrace death and the afterlife — in positive ways that can allow us to transcend the fear of dying?

The 4th Decade of Life

In our thirties we are meant to figure out, if we haven't done it before, how to pay our rent without our parents help. We are meant to finally mature in a way that allows us to actualize a career that expresses our unique life purposes; to develop a primary romantic and intimate relationship; perhaps to have children; and to contribute to the well-being of our society and our earth.

Addressing all of these aspects of life can be challenging, yet ultimately satisfying, as we learn to not only be a part of a love partnership, our own family, and a contributing member of our community but in ways that honor each our uniqueness.

But during this decade how many of us, now as maturing adults, choose to explore spiritual existences beyond life — to embrace death and the afterlife — in positive ways that can allow us to transcend the fear of dying?

The 5th Decade of Life

In our forties...we continue to experience more of the same aspects of self-actualizing and maturing as in our thirties...but we could also continue sometimes to wonder, to ask ourselves, "Where am I, how did I get here? Do I really know who I am? Do I have to exercise so often, detoxify, eat gluten-free even though I love the taste of that pizza wheat dough? I know I'm doing the right things, but I wonder...what else is there, what more is there? Am I doing the right thing? WTF!

But during this decade how many of us are encouraged and/or choose to explore spiritual existences beyond life — to embrace death and the afterlife — in positive ways that can allow us to transcend the fear of dying?

The 6th Decade of Life

In our fifties, we get a sense that maybe we have finally become so wise...from experience, well, from the experiences of screw ups, dissatisfactions as well as peak moments and lasting satisfactions — like finding a partner with whom to share deep love or embracing our aloneness while still responding and interacting to others who care for us. Maybe we have achieved some kind of career accomplishment and/or recognition, but perhaps what's more important, we have found a way to not just obtain a livable income, but to also make enough more to occasionally enjoy traveling and eating out...and enjoying wonderful family times while still finding times for our own personal interests.

We might sometimes get a sense that we know everything. We might be saying to ourselves, "I am so much more mature, and also still have somewhat of a youthful body and spirit and a sound mind. Some say this is the peak of life...Is this the peak of life?"

However, many might also feel a need to find a new purpose or develop a purpose of a long hidden or unrecognized desire, to express ourselves in ways that satisfy something we've always wanted to do and to be. We feel something transforming inside of us, wanting us to let it out, so we can be who we are really meant to be, beyond having and raising children, working at a wage and salary job in a 40-hour week, paying house payments, insurance, and rent. Yes, we've been doing that, now what else? What is the secret treasure within our souls that we are meant to find, appreciate, nurture and share with others?

But during this decade how many of us are encouraged and/or choose to explore spiritual existences beyond life — to embrace death and afterlife — in positive ways that can allow us to transcend the fear of dying?

The 7th Decade of Life

In our sixties, OMG, we feel like we have accomplished a lot, have a sense of maturity and wisdom, and maybe have begun to add those new elements of being that make us feel more complete. But then we are beginning to realize we may not be able to continue to make ends meet. Possible retirement from our wage or salary jobs seem so close, but we are unsure if we will have enough money to live on, to do the things we enjoy doing or have always dreamed of doing. It may become a little more difficult to maintain the health that we are used to.

When we enter our sixties, we are meant to begin a new cycle of maturing that prepares for our eventually passing in positive ways if we haven't done so before. We are meant to open ourselves up to whatever spiritual realities we can embrace — to develop our spiritual maturity that can allow us to have a good death when that time comes.

But during this decade how many of us actually do choose to explore spiritual existences beyond life — to embrace death and afterlife — in positive ways that can allow us to transcend fear the fear of dying?

The 8th Decade of Life

In our seventies, your family and friends might keep saying you look so young, like 20 years younger. That should just piss you off... I mean, you know you don't look like you did in your forties or even fifties...you have gray hair and sometimes forget things, take a lot of medication, and may have arthritis that makes working out often difficult.

Don't get me wrong, in our seventies we can exude a healthy sense of vitality, and we can enjoy our accomplishments, the special memories of our youth, our experiences — and since health consciousness has enabled many of us to maintain good physical health, we can continue to use our skills and knowledge in career and/or avocational ways, and enjoy all the recreational pursuits that give us relaxation and satisfaction.

But during this decade how many of us accept the coming eventuality of our passing and choose to embrace spiritual existences beyond life — to embrace death and the afterlife — in positive ways that can allow us to transcend the fear of dying?

The 9th, 10th, 11th Decades of Life

So in our 80s-90s-100s...why am I combining these years? Whatever got us to our 70s and now is allowing us to live beyond the average lifespan, every moment during these decades could be felt as blessings as long as we can enjoy a quality of life, mental acuity, loving and creative expression, even if it is mixed with some physical pain and the body falling apart — we have to remind ourselves that we are still here, aren't we? And hopefully we have enough of our loved ones and close friends still around to allow us to share memories of the past and create new memories in the present and future.

We will do what we can, try not to be a burden on others, maybe do a little mentoring if anyone will listen to us, and be open to transcending. We can still experience the sparks, the fires that we experienced in the first decades of our lives — and now we know we can take these flames with us to illuminate our way through the coming darkness as we transition into the light of the afterlife. During these decades we will try to embrace everything as we enjoy life and sense what we hope will be a lovely transition.

We might die at any age, in any decade of life, and if we have been exposed to what a good death can be, this awareness can deepen and enhance our thankfulness and ability to live fully in each moment. We can find ourselves at peace, having entered new dimensions of being beyond both the limitations and opportunities of our past lives, structured by the decades and moments of time we have been able to live through, the natural growth and deteriorations of our bodies, the unfolding of our psychological/spiritual being, enhanced by a deep sense of joy, a feeling of a life well lived in the best ways that we are capable of, and as we look forward to the next phases and dimensions of being.

At what age, in what decade in life, have we been prepared or prepared ourselves — by mentoring, by exposure, by choice, by exploration — to experience a good death, whenever that moment of transition comes? Our transition from our earth life can come at any moment in any decade. Why shouldn't we all help each other become more prepared to not just transcend our fears of dying, but to enhance our current lives in ways that would allow us to feel at peace with transcending whenever that time may come?

Spiritually Maturing

G ive me a moment...or maybe a month...maybe a year...ok, perhaps a few decades or maybe even my lifetime or a few more...and then perhaps I'll be mature enough to understand the infinite spiritual meanings of love...and the qualities I need to develop within myself to become more balanced...and my unique potentials I can actualize...and death transitions and the afterlife.

Though I do feel that with the efforts I have made through my life to search for the meanings of various inter-dimensional levels of existence, I have become aware enough to embrace an understanding, appreciation and optimism about the full holistic spectrum of life and the afterlife.

Maturity means understanding holistic patterns of life as well as then making efforts to develop positive connections to the various specific archetypal patterns within our physical realms as well as beyond life dimensions. Maturity is gained through learning from life experiences, as well as by self-study, which requires blending one's rational, abstract and intuitive mentality with an openness to dimensions beyond just evidence-based analysis.

Astrology has identified three cycles of maturity based on age (related to the approximate 29-year cycle of Saturn):

Birth to 28-29 years — Individual Maturing
29 to 59 years — Social-Community Maturing
59 to 88 years — Spiritual Maturing

It is beneficial for individuals to not just focus on maturing in these specific ways of being related to their age and growth in their current lifetimes, but to also focus holistically on developing a mature understanding of what the afterlife means to each of us.

From ages 59 to 88, individuals are meant to continue to develop their maturity related to spirituality in preparation for their own passing into the afterlife, but this focus of maturity hopefully would begin at a younger age since we don't know when our moment of passing will occur.

Discussing Ram Dass With a Cashier at My Local Natural Food Store

In December of 2020, before the New Year began, I went to a local natural food store to buy, among other things, a wall calendar for 2021. I chose a Ram Dass, *Be Here Now Calendar.* I resonated with the sayings as well as the colorful and spiritual photographs for each month.

As I was checking out, the cashier, a woman who seemed to be in her late 20s, held the calendar for a longer moment than usual. She looked at me and said, "I really like this calendar. I appreciate Ram Dass so much." She had curly brown hair, an engaging smile, and it was obvious she enjoyed interacting with customers. Fortunately I was the only one in her line to be checked out.

I said to her that Ram Dass had recently passed, and she said she knew. I told her that during the past year I had read a book he had written with a woman colleague (Mirabai Bush), *Walking Each Other Home-Conversations on Loving and Dying.*

I described the book as containing gentle and profound dialogues between the two spiritual teachers and writings about overcoming fears of death and preparing for a positive dying transition. I said the graphics and format of the book were quite aesthetic and added to the spiritual peace they were trying to convey.

The cashier wrote the title of the book down on a notepad, and said "A few days ago, I saw a documentary about Ram Dass. He talked about how he knew he was dying soon, but felt peaceful about it." She paused for a few moments longer, took a deep breath, and then said, "I'm scared though to think about dying..."

She looked at me for a second, then said, "I need to take a few minutes break. Do you mind if I walk with you to your car?" She didn't wait for my answer but grabbed the "Closed" sign and put it on the counter. She looked at the cashier in the next aisle and said to him, "I'll be back in a few minutes."

She walked around the counter, and walked with me out of the store. She looked at me with a sheepish smile, "I didn't wait for your answer, but I just needed to compose myself. I didn't expect to feel what I am feeling..."

"I don't mind at all," I said. "Did you lose someone recently?

"No, No, not anyone close to me. My mother works as a nurse in the IC unit. During the early part of the COVID, she got sick. She recovered, but she has, I guess, what has been called 'long haul symptoms.' She returned to work, and at first, she shared with me what it was like to care for COVID patients who were dying. It was overwhelming to her, and then to me — how many were dying, the helplessness doctors and nurses were feeling, the aloneness of those who were dying. My mother decided to stop sharing her stories and feelings with me...but what she shared has stayed with me...I guess, affected me in ways that continue to make me uncomfortable and sad...

"I understand...it must be difficult for your mother but I know you must also have felt relieved that she recovered. It seems like many people who are not as close to what's happening in IC units, as you have been with your mother's sharing...many just do not want to focus on the death that's occurring. Our culture does not prepare us for the experience of dying in positive ways, but I believe that being open to exploring death, dying and the afterlife, like you seem to be doing, will bring peace to your life."

"I hope so," she said, and smiled at me. "I will buy that book and share it with my mom." She took a deep breath, and then said, "I've got to get back in...thanks for listening...I feel fortunate to be working in a store like this...the customers are so nice..."

I replied, "As well as the cashiers and customers like you...I appreciate you sharing your experience and feelings with me."

As I drove away from the natural food store, I realized I had not expected her statement about being scared of dying — perhaps because she had been light and communicative at first. Nor had I expected her walking with me to the car and sharing what she did. Then I thought how positive it was, that at her age, she had been open to reading writers and spiritual teachers like Ram Dass and Mirabai Bush, and also was open to expressing to a stranger how scared she was about dying. She seemed like a person who wanted to live life fully and was looking forward to her future on this earth. Her willingness to express her fears represented an initial important phase that could eventually allow her to transcend these fears about dying and death.

If You Die Young...

...know you have lived before and will live again.

I t will be like moving to a new location, only you may have the opportunity to live in different places and to travel to infinite exotic dimensions that will allow you to experience and re-experience comforting and peak spiritual highs.

And your future becomes open and expansive with many other dimensions of being to explore. You never lose touch with your parents, romantic partner and other loved ones and friends...as a matter of spiritual insight, you will experience them in ways that transcend the separateness of your being on earth...you will experience them as you blend with their unique souls, and will be able to touch them in their hearts within their dreams and feelings. You will be with them always...

Time and Inter-dimensional Travel Exists

Each moment is born with unique potentials of being and expression and then dies; that is, it transitions into the birth of a new moment. Actualization of potentials can occur at each moment, but often the actualizations of potentials are spread over dynamic interconnections of moments evolving through phases and cycles of time...until the final moment of transitioning from our bodies in the earth realm into essences of being beyond time in beyond life dimensions. We can create our own future realities. We can travel into inter-dimensional states of consciousness during which we can see into possible futures. And then we can decide which future we want to attempt to create.

Eventually we will be able to physically travel through time — threads of past and future — as we live in our current earth bodies, but until technological potentials catch up with spiritual actualities, we can travel through time and dimensions within our transpersonal consciousness. We cannot only create our future realities as we experience inter-dimensional beyond time travel, we can become more prepared for an exciting transition into the afterlife...

What Do You Want to Accomplish in Your Life Before You Die?

In my late 20's — many years ago (but I still remember some things about those years), when I was studying various psychological and metaphysical systems, I was asked to write an essay answering this question by one of my teachers.

As I answered this question, I knew I must have written about my search for love and to connect with a love partner...to feel that I could express my love in flowing, respectful, responsive, passionately interactive and in uninhibited ways that encourage each of our own realizations of our potentials.

I know I must have expressed the desire to interact with unconditional love, presence and appropriate guidance as a parent and step-parent with the children whom I would be fortunate to experience as a part of my life. These relationships would involve blood connections and transcend blood connections.

I know I must have written about my hope to continue writing and maybe publishing poetry, stories, drama, and my developing awareness of the holistic models of life (based upon astrology and the psychological theories of Carl Jung) that I was becoming aware of and resonating with.

I know I must have expressed the wish to travel, especially to places like Europe, Toronto, New Orleans, and perhaps to some warm beach areas.

I have to admit I didn't indicate, at my young age, that I wanted to be able to open myself experientially to dimensions of beyond life and the afterlife. That came many years later — actually just a few years ago...but I do feel fortunate that it happened before my time of transitioning to the afterlife...and that I've been able to take advantage of this spiritual awareness to revise what I want to accomplish in my life before I die.

I'm Studying Death

H ow have you been?" she asked him, so caringly, when she ran into him on the street by the university bookstore. She had not seen or heard from him since they amicably broke up and she moved away a couple of years prior. She had come back to town a few days ago to visit a woman friend and was taking a walk around the university area where she had graduated.

"I'm fine," he said, with what seemed to her like a cursory smile. She did not let this bother her. She knew of his sometimes-reluctance to open up right away.

"What are you doing now?" she asked with sincere curiosity.

"Oh, I'm studying death..." he said in what seemed to her such a matter-of-fact way of describing a topic that has such a dramatic impact...at least for her.

She hesitated, and stared silently into his eyes for a moment, not knowing what to say...Then she asked, "You are studying death?" She had not known how else to respond.

"Yes. Haven't you ever been...concerned about dying, or affected by the death of a loved one or a dear friend?"

"Well...yes..." But she realized she hadn't really ever wanted to pursue these thoughts...or feelings.

"Haven't you ever then wondered — wanted to know about what's going on with people who have passed, or what will go on with you in the afterlife?"

"We'll never know..." she responded.

"We will never know until we enter the afterlife, but what if we can know before we pass... What if I am dead now and talking with you from another dimension?"

She began to worry, "What's going on with him...?" She felt uncomfortable about what was happening. She had thought her reaching out to him would just be a brief "hello" and catching up. She finally responded, "But you are not dead…"

"Yet"

"What does that mean…are you ok…you seem so strange in what you are talking about?" She had actually begun to feel irritated, but pushed that feeling aside because she realized that maybe something not good might be going on with him. She had a scary thought that he might be thinking about killing himself.

"I've just realized that it's not emotionally healthy to ignore and not prepare for our own deaths in positive and spiritual ways. I believe we all need to expand our ideas of what goes on in dimensions after death and while we are alive, how we can connect with these dimensions and those essences who have passed into these dimensions…"

"WOW, I didn't expect you would be talking about this subject…I mean, I do value spiritual practices…I just haven't thought about connecting it so much to dying or death. We're only in our 30s."

He paused for a moment, and then smiled as if coming out of a trance… "I'm sorry I'm being so serious here…but I just think it's important for us living at any age to study…well, reflect on, what a good death is…and what comes after — beyond what religion has fed us." He paused again, but then asked," Do you have time to have a coffee with me…and I promise, I won't talk anymore about death."

She also smiled, relieved that he was coming out of a weird and serious space, and remembered how much she enjoyed his lightness. "Yes, I have time to get a cup of coffee. That would be nice." Then she surprised herself as she said, "Though I guess I would like to talk more about your study of death and the afterlife. I just haven't thought about these things and I was feeling strange and uncomfortable at first as you talked so seriously …and what seemed so impersonally. I was worried about you until I saw your smile, but now I'm feeling something meaningful is happening here. I want to know more."

He continued to smile and said, "I'm open to sharing more about my studies…and also I want to catch up with what's been going with you…we haven't seen each other for so long…I've thought about you so often."

Most of Us Are Not Prepared to Die...

...because many of us do not want to talk about dying in our "go-go", capitalistic society where life is profit and profit is life...and as many of us choose to keep going, going, going, hoping for the best, hoping for success, and as Dylan Thomas wrote, "Rage, Rage against the dying of the light".

I believe it is essential for us to embrace the light of life in our current human form, but it is also beneficial for us to embrace the light of the afterlife...and learn that it is not something to fear...that we can be prepared to let go when we have to let go, and that dying is not something to fear. Let the feeling of fear and resistance be acknowledged and then let this feeling be transformed into an appreciation of each moment of life.

We have to prepare ourselves because, so far, our society is so much in a death denial mode, and that leads to fear, a lack of spiritual preparation for a transition that we will all experience.

Why is our society wanting us to deny this life transition that we all will experience? I guess there are many reasons why, but the important resolution for each of us to make is to begin the effort to develop a spiritual sense of well-being within us that includes, not just an acceptance, but a joyful anticipation of one day moving into the wonderment of the afterlife.

Why Do We Resist Dying?

We resist dying because we have the fires of life burning in the center of our being — we have a purpose in this life and we are born to actualize these potentials, to bring to a fulfillment our unique potentials as best we can. We have streaming lavas of love, of hope, of dreams, of accomplishments, of purpose...streams that spread emotionally out through our consciousness and onto the paths on the earth we walk...streams of unique potentials that we hope will form the future of what we want to actualize with our fiery essences while we remain alive.

We resist dying, because from the time of our births we are meant to flourish our unique potentials through the seasons of existence year after year...

We resist dying because we have forgotten the spiritual womb we came from before we were nurtured in our mother's womb...

We resist dying because we have forgotten that we belong to nurturing dimensions that encompass the existence in the current life we are born into, the existence structured by the day and night, by the interplay of light and darkness that unfolds year after year through the seasons of our life on earth...

We resist dying because we have forgotten we belong to something larger, more caring, healing and embracing than our existence during our time on earth.

We resist dying because, in our western culture, our individual purposes and urges to be have been severed from the awareness of such spiritual resources that can provide us strength, courage and ease of spirit as we face the struggles of life, and that allows us to put into perspective our accomplishments and the eventual transition of death that brings us home, back to dimensions that allow us to spread our being beyond what we know and into possibilities of joyful being beyond our dreams.

We are right to build our fires of being in the earth realm, of making concrete our purposes, of living life to the fullest. We are meant to build our uniqueness as we develop our maturity — yet it is unfortunate that we do this at the expense of making peace, embracing and making preparations for our passing back home into the spiritual dimensions where we have come from.

Death Phobia

I s it death you fear, or it is the pain you might feel as you die? Is it losing your connections with your love ones? Or is it losing everything you worked for in your life? Or is it...not wanting to leave sensual earthly pleasures? Or is it traveling into the unknown, away from your security "blankets" you've encased yourself in to give you feelings of well-being?

Some of you have chosen to develop yourselves beyond your own subjective sense of security, and have opened yourself to a spiritual security that will help you to transcend insecurities, as you live your life, and as you die.

You will die one moment in time and transcend into the afterlife. Those who are agoraphobic may have aversion about going outside their houses. Not to minimize their fears, but it seems beneficial for all of us to transcend our fears of leaving our place of earthly security, and our bodies, our lives, our emotional homes during our current lifetime...because we have no choice, which makes it spiritually and emotionally beneficial to transcend our death phobias.

Wily Wizard's Death Guidance

Wily Wizard studied his crystal ball, occasionally looking up at the 29-year-old woman who was sitting before him. He could see she was disconcerted, nervous, and he felt concerned about her fear of dying.

Actually, the Wily Wizard was not focusing on the crystal ball...he already had identified the many ways she could die, the many ways she could leave this earth to enter into the wondrous dimensions of the afterlife, depending on certain choices she might make.

Wily Wizard could not tell her what he was seeing — all the many ways she could die. Instead he chose to spread the wonderment of the transcendental visions — comforting hues and tones of colors, creating inspiring visions of the afterlife throughout the room and within her psyche.

Then he reached across the table as she entered a sense of spiritual well-being and put his hand on hers. He said as her eyes glowed with joy, "Be at peace. Nobody ever really dies."

Enhancing Your Life's Desires by Embracing Your Eventual Death

E mbracing your coming death and making peaceful, conscious connections with the afterlife dimensions, no matter your age and state of health, will enhance your desires to experience life with passion while you are living out your sparks of life:

Your desire to live each moment to the fullest

Your desire to overcome your fears and anxieties about dying and death

Your desire to overcome the grieving of loss

Your desires to accept and love who you are at any given moment, even while you continue to strive to yourself and develop your special unique potentials while you are living

Your desires to fully experience love and intimacy while sharing your life's desires.

Almost Dying in Car Crashes

I have almost died twice in car crashes. One when I was about 17 years old. A friend and I were driving from Calgary, Alberta to Houston, Texas in December in more than 20 degrees below zero weather. When my friend who was driving hit an ice patch, the small Renault Dauphine slid off the highway and rolled through the air. When it landed, I was upside down in the driver's seat and my friend was in the passenger seat — the only reason we were saved was because the engine was in the back of the car where only that part of the roof was smashed in.

The other Accident occurred in 1987, when I was 43 years old, and driving a work colleague's car (a new Honda Accord) from Eugene to Portland on a nice sunny day.

All of a sudden, a semi-trailer truck came across the median from the other side of the highway, right in front of our car. I didn't have any time to swerve but just braked a little and slid down a bit in my seat. Our car crashed into the truck going 65 miles per hour. We were fortunate that we smashed into the truck exactly in the space between its front and rear wheels.

As we crashed, the car somehow passed underneath the truck between the wheels. As our car passed underneath the truck, the roof was torn off but we ended up on the other side of the truck, both alive. I was unconscious briefly but the only injury I sustained was when the visor attached to the roof partially ripped my left ear, which later was sewed back on at the hospital.

My work colleague was not physically injured. Some people called hitting the truck exactly between the wheels a miracle. Others teased me that maybe I should become a stunt driver.

How did I survive these experiences of nearly dying in crashes? There was nothing I could have done — I was just cosmically fortunate, I guess. After each accident, I got back into the rush of life right away, not thinking much about how close I had been to being killed, not thinking much about how close I had been to entering the afterlife. But these experiences of almost dying have stayed with me over the years, buried within my psyche waiting for acknowledgement and a different kind of conscious resurrection that will lead to a fuller connection to beyond life dimensions.

As He Was Dying in a Sudden Car Accident

He was listening to one of his favorite podcasts and driving within the speed limit, when a van swerved into his lane, crashing into his car, causing it to careen off the highway. He died instantly as his head was crushed by the roof of the car...and he was surprised that he suddenly became aware of what had happened, and as he was drifting away, he could see his smashed car but felt detached from it and his body inside...receding, receding...

And then he remembered what had happened. He felt no pain, but strangely felt a sense of liberation, though he did not want to leave his wife and child, who were the joys of his life. He initially felt a deep sense of sorrow at leaving his family whom he loved. He had been driving home from working out of town, and was bringing home his wife's favorite flowers and a toy for his child. He remembered these gifts which at first deepened his sorrow...

Yet he also began to feel a different kind of joy...a joy that seemed to be washing away his sorrow, and he found himself feeling a purpose of being beyond anything that he had experienced before in his past existence...he began to understand he would not be apart from his wife and his child and others whom he loved...he would be connecting with them in spiritually fulfilling ways.

He realized he would be expanding into dimensions beyond his dreams, yet would be able to remain connected with his wife and child in their dreams while they continued their lives on earth...and he would remain connected in other ways, through communications that come through memories, as they remembered what they had experienced together, and also as they make future choices based upon the values and guiding principles of the life he has shared with them.

He knew he was and was not leaving them behind...he just hoped as they grieved his loss, they would eventually be able to rise above their sorrows and feel the same spiritual joys that he was now feeling. And he knew that he would be able to help them in this process of transforming their grieving. He imagined himself smiling as on he continued to drift joyfully into afterlife dimensions.

When I Die — Falling Through Cracks

Will I feel I'm falling through cracks in the physical realities of the earth realm? Will I feel I'm falling into a soft net, not feeling scared, while being caressed and embraced by the beyond life dimensions — by the warm and inviting light...

I hope to realize that somewhere in this transition I'll be aware that I am dissolving into what seems like infinite dimensions of joy...aware that my unique consciousness is also connected and aware of all essences of being...even if I don't know the specifics of what everyone is doing, I will feel their souls, their essences and this will comfort me, enhance me, make me much more than who I was and will expand me into more than I am...ever falling through the cracks of the limits of the earth and other physical realms.

Wily Wizard Facilitates a Fear of Death Support Group

Wily Wizard, as the facilitator, sat with 8 other people, all in their chairs in a circle in a room that was non-descript, meaning, well, meaning a bit bland.

None of the participants knew Wily Wizard came from beyond life dimensions. When he visits the earth realm, which he does more often than he likes to admit, he generally chooses not to share what he calls his lack of identity, but also has not hid the fact he's a bit weird. He hoped none of the other participants would notice he had a wily streak in him, yet he soon realized those gathered around him were more consumed with their own concerns and fears than with him. He sincerely wanted to help them transcend their fear of dying and death, and he believed that humor and nonsense were the best ways of doing that. Yet, he knew with his wizardry wisdom that not everyone can laugh through their fears. Though, he believed that was because they just haven't heard the right joke...

Instead of tie-dyed clothing that he usually liked to wear in the earth realm, he was wearing casual, loose pants and a loose shirt with a design on the front of a man and a woman laughing.

When he was alone, the design became an animation of the man and woman tickling each other which he felt also, and he enjoyed the light giggling touches — yet he felt the general public could not yet understand how such designs to shirts could move, and he was worried he would be badgered with questions of where a shirt like his could be bought, which of course, it couldn't be.

Wily Wizard even trimmed his beard, well, he imagined that his beard was trimmed and it just was...another one of the many infinite advantages of existing in the beyond life dimension. He also still wore his glowing, inter-dimensional necklace beneath his shirt to make sure nobody would notice and become distracted.

When everyone was seated, Wily turned to Sharon, 58-years-old, and asked her if she would begin. Sharon took a deep breath. She shared that she was afraid that when she died, she would be forced to reincarnate as a frog. She said that from the time she was a young child, she loved eating frog legs, and has only lately begun to feel guilty, yet she just loved the taste and texture of frog legs. She said that when she was growing up in the south of Texas, one of her uncles would take her out into the swamps and they would catch frogs by shining lights into their eyes, which caused them to freeze in place, and then either she or her uncle would reach out from the boat they were sitting in and grab them and put them in a bag. Afterwards, when they returned to land, she and her uncle would skin and then cook them.

She always considered them such a delicacy.

As she talked, tears began to form in her eyes, and as she looked at Wily, she said she didn't want be reincarnated as a frog, as she had begun to fear she would be...she wondered if it was her karma.

After she finished, Wily told her that his research in reincarnation, karma, the afterlife doctrines and ir-realities (he hoped nobody would notice his slip of the tongue) indicated that coming back as a frog is a step up above humanity.

"What?" she asked, confused.

"Yes, frogs are really princes and princesses and even transgenders or beyond genders. Over centuries, they have given their croaking sounds and some, like you would say, "delicious legs", to humans as precious spiritual sounds and delicacies of food for the spiritually needy. So, Sharon, coming back as a frog would be an honor...but there is more to this. In my studies I have understood that you would still have a choice in what form or essence you would return to in the physical realms, if you even choose to do so. And besides frogs don't live that long, so you'll be back in the afterlife in no time — or in a relatively little time — and will be able to make another choice, if you so choose."

Wily Wizard could tell Sharon was still processing what he had said. He waved his invisible, magical wand and evoked feelings of peace within her psyche. He did not want to do this before he shared knowledge of the afterlife that he felt people he came into contact on earth should know. But then he had realized that since most people on earth had only so much time in a relative sense to live, why not give them peace and laughter in a hurry — though generally after he has shared his knowledge with them.

Wily Wizard looked at the others and said, "Ok, who's next?"

Chad, 68-years-old, said he worried about being in a lot of pain when he died.

Wily asked, "What is the worst pain you fear?"

"I fear any pain at all, and I already feel pain all the time," Chad responded looking quite distraught.

"What about pain medication?" Wily Wizard asked.

"I already take a lot of pain medication and it still doesn't help."

"What do you take the pain medications for and who prescribes them for you?"

"I take pain medications for my fears of feeling pain, and nobody prescribes them...I admit I get them from friends and family."

Wily invisibly reached inside Chad's psyche and tickled him and Chad started giggling and then laughing uncontrollably. His laughter was contagious, and everyone started laughing also, not realizing that Wily Wizard was also invisibly tickling them.

After a moment, when Wily Wizard stopped tickling their psyches and the laughter died down (I mean, transitioned down), Wily Wizard asked Chad how he was feeling.

Chad looked shocked and said, "I'm in no pain! What happened?"

"Just the release of laughter...that's all the pain relief that you need."

"But how do I continue laughing? I don't usually feel like laughing."

Wily Wizard reached into his pack, took out a tattered paperback book and handed it to Chad.

"Here's some jokes I have collected and some I have written over time. Read some of these when you get up in the morning, and at other times during the day and before you go to bed, and I guarantee you will always have a smile on your face. You will begin to feel whatever pain you might be feeling is transitory and can be relieved by entering into the realm of nonsense, which is another way of describing some of what goes on in the afterlife. Use joke books like these as your pain relief medication...it's sort of natural and organic in a spiritual sense, no toxic put downs or belittling jokes are used.

Wily Wizard then turned to Selena, and asked if she wanted to share. Selena was 29 years old, and had shared before that she still lives with her parents, whom she loves deeply.

Selena began, "I just fear dying...everything about dying...I don't even like leaving my home very often. I've been diagnosed with Agoraphobia."

Wily Wizard responded, "Selena, when you die, you don't have to leave your home." He turned to the group, "Listen everyone, when you die you have choices." Then he repeated, "You will have CHOICES in beyond life dimensions."

He turned back to Selena and said, "Selena, you can always choose to hang around as a ghost for as long as you would like, but I want you to know that when you actually transcend into afterlife, you will feel just like you do when you are at home in the earth realm and that's what many people don't realize. In beyond life dimensions, you can and are everywhere...and yet anywhere specific you choose to be."

The group looked confused again. "Imagine that you have 100 smartphones set all around your room, and you are alone, and yet you are able to connect with 100 different people in 100 different places — that might be confusing to your earth psyches, but imagine you can focus on who and where you want, and still feel connected to all the other people and places, and bring them into the main focus when you wanted to..."

He saw that he was losing them, especially Selena. He turned to her again, and said, "Selena, I just want to emphasize again that if you want to remain home after you transcend, you can...but if you do that, you need to be nice to those who are still living in the earth realm...be a sweet and caring ghost, not a demanding and mean one...and I just want you to know that when you are ready to enter the beyond life dimension fully you will feel just as at home."

Selena nodded, and said she felt relieved.

Paul, 77-years-old, was the next to share, "I don't want to leave my wife, kids and grandkids — and I have a great grandchild coming in about six months. Yet, I have been diagnosed with cancer that fortunately is in early stages, and after my surgery, the treatment seems to be going well. Of course, I'm thinking often about dying and leaving my loved ones. I'm feeling a deep and painful sadness about that, and sometimes I feel it as a fear...of losing the connection with those I love so much."

Wily Wizard turned to others in the group, "Does anyone in the group have a response to Paul's concerns?"

Everyone was silent for a moment. Then Carol, the youngest member of the group at 21-years-old said, "I almost died last year in a car accident, and I had a near-death experience. For the time I was considered dead, I can remember existing somewhere I can only describe as being peaceful and lovely, and I was being caressed by my father who had died when I was young. I also felt caressed by others, some I later learned were ancestors of our family. I learned that my father and the others had always been present with me, and that they would also be waiting for me when my time came to actually leave this world. I was somehow brought back to life, but this experience has seemed to remain with me as a glow of peace that relieves my fear of death."

Paul responded, "Thanks for sharing that experience with me. I've read about near-death experiences, but hearing what you experienced personally gives me some relief. But can I ask you a question?"

"Sure."

"You said you don't have a fear of dying or death. Why are you here?"

Carol smiled and hesitated, but then said, "After what I experienced, I want to lead groups like this, and I've been studying, attending various workshops, and meeting healers. I found a flyer at a coffee shop near my house that advertised this support group, and for some reason as I looked at the poster, I started laughing, and felt a sense of joy that was like what I felt when I had my near-death experience. I took the flyer home and every time I looked at it, I felt the same joy, and found myself giggling. So I became curious. I know it sounds strange, but being in this group I also feel this happiness and joy about the afterlife even more — and in a sort of light-hearted way."

Paul said, "I also have to say that just being here in this group has made me feel more at peace about my coming passing. Yet now I am feeling a bit of guilt about being ok with dying and leaving my loved ones."

Wily responded, "Don't feel guilt for feeling at peace about moving on...besides guilt or all those non-helpful feelings do not exist in the afterlife."

Paul said that made him feel more at peace, but then asked if he could have one of those flyers that Carol had found. He said that he wondered if he would experience the same effect.

Wily Wizard said that he would give out flyers to anyone who might want them after the meeting, and smiled to himself as he thought about the potions of joy and nonsensical laughter he had sprinkled over the flyers.

He said, "Ok who's next..."

Phyllis said, "Death has always been depicted as a being in a black robe ready to end your life with a swipe of his scythe and pull you into darkness. Or as a horrible creature with huge jaws and sharp teeth, or as a red devil about to pull me down into hell..."

"Stop! You are scaring me," Wily Wizard interrupted feigning a fearful face. The other participants in the group gasped.

Then Wily Wizard laughed, and said, "Just kidding. But please understand that making light of those images of fear you are expressing is not to minimize them, but to...well, to shine the light of illumination that shows how nonsensical they are in relation to what is really involved in transcending into beyond life dimensions and what the afterlife is all about. It is important to realize that transcending into the afterlife is an experience we will all have, and it is truly one of joy and lightness and not to be feared. Those images come from humans who have always tried to control others for their own purposes. And believe me, most of them did not, and do not, have a sense of spiritual joy or humor. By the way, when people transcend into the afterlife, the first things they experience are joy and laughter and they realize how harmful as well as nonsensical these human attempts to perpetuate such fears have been."

Morris, a 53-year-old man, was the next to share, "I want to commit suicide, but I'm afraid of death."

"But what's your problem?" Wily Wizard asked.

"I just told you. I want to die, but I'm afraid of the experience of dying."

"Well, it seems like you might have some beyond life essences who don't want you to leave your life on earth right now. But I will give you few specific meditations and visualizations to see if you can resolve your dilemma."

"Medications?" he asked hopefully.

"No, *meditations* that will help you dissolve your fear of death. These meditations will not only relieve your desire to die, but will prepare you for dying peacefully when that happens."

Morris looked perplexed.

Wily Wizard continued, "You are experiencing a conundrum — it's your fear of death that is frustrating your death wish. Don't ask me to explain...I don't understand it either, but just be happy because you are really in a win-win situation. You can continue to enjoy living, and yet if you do take your own earth life, you will find that your transition will be fine. But I don't recommend you taking your own life, unless you have a good spiritual reason.

"Ok, one last sharing."

Rick volunteered, "I don't know why, but lately, I've been having these dreams that I am being fried to death as a hamburger, sometimes a garden burger, on a grill in a fast-food restaurant. And I have this irrational fear of dying in that way. I know it sounds crazy."

Wily Wizard thought that for sure that this sounded really crazy and ridiculous — another food issue related to the fear of dying. He decided, though, that this was a perfect way to end this session of the support group. Then he wondered what he could say to assist in relieving Rick's fears that this dream was causing him.

"Rick, do you like eating in fast food restaurants?"

"Yes, given my work schedules, I eat in all sorts of hamburger and chicken fast food places..."

Wily Wizard thought for a moment, and finally said, "Just be thankful and find peace in the realization that if that dream really came true, your passing would go fast since you were being fried in a fast food restaurant — just think if you were in a higher end gourmet restaurant in which you were being marinated and stewed over hours and hours...look Rick, we have to sometimes find peace in crazy ways...just relax about those dreams — oh, and maybe you might want to stop eating in fast food restaurants so often — that probably will help you live longer anyway. Your psyche or some essence in beyond life dimensions was probably concerned about your eating habits and was trying to scare you into eating better. Nothing really to fear though..."

Wily Wizard looked around the group and said, "Ok, that's enough for today. Everyone stand up and start dancing in as crazy of a way as you can imagine as we move around in a circle...and take a wild sense of nonsense and silliness with you as leave...

Is This My Last Day on Earth?

COVID — I'm lying in a bed without my family around as I am trying to hold onto life, breathing on a ventilator...but I wish I could hold my loved one's hands...

TERMINAL ILLNESS — I am dying of a chronic illness and I have been told it's not my fault that I developed this terminal illness. There is so much toxicity in our environment and we all are vulnerable to genetic vulnerabilities. Maybe I could have done better in my life style, but feel I have done the best I could, and as I pass, I just want to hold your hand, feel your touch...

UNFORESEEN EVENTS — In the split second I am aware of something I can't control and that I know will kill me, I just hope my loved ones know I will never leave them as I journey into the afterlife, and though I won't be able to hold their hands as I transition, I will hold them in my soul, in their souls...

ABUSED AND UNRESTRAINED AGGRESSION — As I experienced the act of aggression that will kill me, I want everyone to know that I didn't deserve this harm...and I'm going to miss being with my child, my parents...and I can't think about forgiveness yet, but maybe as I transition into the afterlife, I may be able to embrace that feeling for the person who has fully abused and killed me...now I just wish I could let those who love me know that I am peaceful and ok.

INTO THE UNKNOWN — I don't know what happened. One minute I'm baking bread and the next awareness I'm in this amazing wonderful essence of existence. I don't know where I am, and yet

I'm feeling I'm in the place I should be even if I don't yet know where this is...I have a sense that it is not a place, it's not a "whereness", it's beyond what I've known, and I'm feeling for the first time in my essence of being that I'm excited to enter into the unknown...

What Is the Purpose of Imagining How You Might Die?

Will you die walking across the street not looking both ways as a fast car is driving past? The purpose of imagining from time to time the different ways you might die...realizing that there are many ways to die...is not to cause anxiety about how and when you will die. The purpose and benefit of reflecting about the process of dying, the different possibilities, is to transcend our anxieties about death and dying.

Does thinking about how you might die seem unrelated to other special aspects of your life? The joys of love of romance, family and friendship, the accomplishments of your unique endeavors in life — are these unrelated to how we prepare to die a good death?

It is important to make peace with death — not as a way of bringing anxiety into our emotional states of being, or at least hanging onto these anxieties. We need to make peace with our coming death, with courage, as a way of reminding ourselves to take advantage of every moment we are living. Taking advantage of our life moments does not mean that we always have to be doing something — we don't always have to be busy, to continually strive. We can balance our goal-oriented actions with resting, meditating, reflecting, imagining — taking a nap in the middle of the day, strolling along aimlessly through the city in which we live, or in nature...

It is important for each of us to connect with beyond life dimensions while we are alive as a way of preparing for our time to enter fully into these dimensions.

The act of reflecting occasionally on the ways we might die should not be an end in itself, just as death is not an end in itself...reflecting on how we might die, just as all thoughts about death, should be a reminder of the preciousness of life as well as the afterlife.

I Know You Don't Want to Die

Listening to a friend share his desires for living and his fears about dying:

I have so much I want to do in my life... I don't care what age I am (though that makes some difference when I might die), but let's say I am young, in my 20s, 30s, 40s, 50s, 60s, even 70s - well even 80s and 90s — let's put those years there too because, maybe I'll be a bit bionic by the time I reach those years...maybe be part AI, but I still may have a human life force within my psyche...

I don't want to die because...

I want to meet the love of my life, if I haven't met the love of my life;

If I have met the love of my life, I want to experience years of us making love passionately and fulfilling both of our desires and need for intimate sharing;

I want to have children and grandchildren and great-grandchildren, and experience years of caring for them, doting on them, feeling love from them, seeing them become the unique and special beings they were meant to be as they grew into adults and developed their uniqueness of beings;

I want to travel to places in the world that give me pleasure, relaxation, adventure, surprises and help me understand the wonderful diversity of humanity and other life forms, or at least where there are warm beaches;

I want to enjoy life... I will always want to have more time to enjoy life no matter how old I am, as long as I can enjoy some parts of life, even if I'm in a nursing home — well, I do hope that my caregivers will be nice to me — I'm sure they will be. I'm optimistic about life and will always hope for the best;

I don't want to die as long as I still have this optimism and hope for the future. I do wish I could bring this feeling of optimism and hope as I think about dying and transitioning into the afterlife.

I want to enjoy life no matter how old I am —
I might have 40 years of life if I am 40 years old;

I might have 30 years of life if I am 50 years old;

I might have 10 years of life if I'm 70 years old.

Maybe I have only one year of life left no matter how old am. Maybe six months. Maybe just a day. Maybe just a moment...the next moment...a car will hit me, I will have a heart attack, I will choke on something I'm eating, I...

I'M NOT PREPARED TO DIE!!!!!!!!!!!!!!!!!!!!!
WHY AM I NOT PREPARED TO DIE? WHAT'S WRONG WITH THE SOCIETAL CULTURE I AM LIVING IN THAT HAS NOT PREPARED ME PEACEFULLY TO DIE. IT'S GOING TO HAPPEN. I WILL DIE. WHY AM I NOT PREPARED FOR IT?

I know I need to take responsibility for preparing for my spiritual development, and for preparing for peacefully dying whenever that may occur. But I do blame my society that hides death away, doesn't want to expose the young, and even older adult's to death. Why not? Because I have been conditioned to believe that life is all that matters, it seems — not the spiritual afterlife.

Make Peace With Death

Responding to my friend's fear of dying

I know you want to make peace with death. You tell me you are working on it...though you say you're not there yet...you smile at least and say you mean you're not dying yet...then you become serious again, and say, *not that I know of...*but you say again that you have not yet made peace with death and that you are working on it...because you've come to realize, at least intellectually, that death is not a loss of the wonders of what we know of life...but a transition into dimensions of wonders beyond what we know...you say you just want to make peace with this transition...not to fear it...not to resist when it happens or is supposed to happen.

Yet until it happens, yes, you want to resist dying in affirmative ways...affirming the joys of living in this earth realm, while also being open to the joys waiting in the coming afterlife...whenever it might come...and as you close your eyes and take a deep breath and say you will keep working on it...focus on the connection between the glowing sunset of life (whenever that occurs at any age) and the beautiful bright light of the dawn of the afterlife...

Take Deep Breaths When You Become Anxious About Dying

You say you feel anxious when thinking about death...your own death...or those you love. You say you try not to think about dying, but it just happens...these thoughts just come into your mind sometimes, and you feel overwhelmed, fearful.

When this happens try sitting comfortably in your chair or lay down on your sofa or bed. Begin taking a few deep breaths, drawing these breaths from the lower part of your abdomen, holding the breath for a few seconds, focusing on the breath of life, renew and affirm that you are living fully in the moments. Then as you slowly release your breath, imagine that your essence of being is floating into a new dimension with joy, with peace, and then imagine that you are feeling exhilarated. You are feeling as though you are being reborn with your awareness and consciousness, and then realize you are still connected to your past life, the life you are leaving...and you have nothing to fear because what you fear as dying is actually allowing your consciousness to be transformed, expand and you will be experiencing a spiritual joy you were not fully able to feel even as you experience the joys of living and loving while you were in your earth body.

Just take a few more deep breaths, and as you do imagine you are lying on a sunny beach...with the sounds of ocean waves soothing you and inviting you to come into the warm and refreshing waters where you can swim among wonders beneath the surfaces without needing to breathe.

You're right, our culture does not prepare us for dying. Just as most births occur in hospitals, most deaths are hidden away from families these days, as most individuals pass not in their homes, but in sterile, mostly white hospital rooms hooked up to tubes and IVs and surrounded by caring nurses, doctors but still mostly strangers.

So you will feel anxious at times...we are not prepared to die.

Try taking a few more deep breaths and imagine that when you die you are lying in your bed with your love ones surrounding you and also surrounded by those people and caregivers you feel close to.

Imagine music and candlelight and incense surrounding and caressing you, helping you feel embraced and comforted, not just by those who love you, but also something that is just beyond your consciousness — essences of being, spiritual nurturance...and let your breaths comfort you as you enter into dimensions on the last spiritual breath you take that will take you to afterlife dimensions where your soul transcends the need to breathe.

Spiritual Visualizations — Gerald's Beginning Connection to Beyond Life Dimensions...

One morning 35-year-old Gerald lay in his bed before getting up, as he tried to consciously meditate for the first time in his life (that he knew of).

This was something he had never tried before, but he had read science fiction and fantasy all his life and had just read a book about a character who received guidance from spirits that helped him overcome devastating feelings of loss from the death of a woman he considered the love of his life.

During the past few years Gerald had felt the growing need to understand more about spiritual aspects of life. He was not raised with any religious connections from his family, but his mother and father were into spiritual New Age practices related to such things as shamanism and astrology, which he always considered weird and nothing he wanted to learn about or become involved in. Yet as he grew older and especially as he entered into his thirties, he began to realize his exposure to these spiritual practices of his parents had somehow planted seeds within him that had begun to flower.

Gerald had recently been in a relationship that ended in a way that had been quite devastating to him. His woman friend, Emma, was different than any woman he had previously been with, and he had fallen deeply in love with her. They had been planning to move into together. They had enjoyed each other's company in both passionate and spontaneous ways, but then she had become interested in exploring spiritual practices such as meditation, and to his shock and discomfort Emma began to spend a great deal of time with his parents during which they discussed metaphysical and spiritual practices and concepts.

Emma tried to share her thoughts about these concepts with him, but after she broke off the relationship, he realized that he had not been willing to at least respect her beliefs. He realized that he had not only been closed to her beliefs, he had often made light of them in disrespectful ways.

After she broke up with him, he had spent most of his time alone trying to adjust to his feelings of loss. He felt no desire to engage in another romantic or intimate relationship, and he dove into his books and his work. He had become an engineering tech and the surety of the technical data and calculations gave him peace for a while. However at one point he realized he was not feeling content most of the time.

He finally decided he needed counseling and began seeing a Jungian therapist, who wanted to help him understand his dreams, but he told her he didn't normally remember his dreams. She taught him techniques to help him remember his dreams, which he was surprised worked. He began to remember his dreams each night, and some of them were quite amazing to him — full of imaginative flights of fancy and imagery that at first, he did not understand.

His sessions with his therapist became quite meaningful to him, and his sense of loss began to ease. He began to realize how closed-minded he had been. His counselor helped him to not stay in feelings of self-criticism or guilt, but to realize he was growing and becoming more open to areas of life and spirituality that he had closed himself off from. She encouraged him to appreciate the new inner journey he was taking.

At one point, his Jungian-oriented therapist suggested he try meditation, and taught him breathing techniques to try if he chose to pursue this practice. She also taught him the concept of synchronicity, in which meaningful coincidences can be special gateways to enhance psychological and spiritual understanding and growth.

When he read the science fiction novel about the main character who sought connection with the spiritual world and received guidance that helped him overcome the death of his wife, he decided he was ready to try meditative techniques to see if he could open himself up to spiritual realms.

He had not yet told anyone, especially his parents, about his new explorations into psychological and spiritual realms.

Gerald lay on his back in a comfortable position, and began to breathe deeply from his stomach and focused on his inhaled breath as it filled his lungs. He continued to breathe, inhaling and exhaling, and focused on how various parts of his body felt, and when he noticed tensions, he imagined his breath flowing into the part of the body to release the tension — just as his therapist had guided him to do.

At one point he began to visualize himself looking down at his body from a distance above. He visualized his bed and his body lying in the bed. He watched himself as he breathed in and out rhythmically — he noticed that the room itself had disappeared, and he could only see himself lying in the bed with his eyes closed breathing rhythmically in and out...

Then from his view above, Gerald began to visualize white translucent cloud-like substances flowing into his space and surrounding him as he lay meditating on his bed. He watched the white cloud-like substances fully surround him, and at one point he found himself back in his body breathing deeply and rhythmically with his eyes closed, not only feeling but also visualizing the white essences caressing his consciousness. Then the substances began to dissolve, and as they did, he found himself entering into another dimension where there were human-shaped beings seemingly floating all around him, greeting him. He did not recognize who these beings were, but felt peaceful in their presence...

He then saw Emma in the distance and called to her. She turned his way and smiled and floated up to him. She said to him without words, "I wondered if you would ever make it here."

"What is here?" Gerald said. "Isn't this the afterlife? But you are not dead."

She smiled again, "No I am not, and you are not dead either, silly. You have just entered into beyond life dimensions just as I have been able to do in my own spiritual practices. I'm happy you have opened yourself up to this dimension, and it is quite amazing that you have been able to dissolve — evolve into this dimension with your early tries. This is not the afterlife, but it's all one and the same, and by using the practices you are being taught, you will become familiar with what it will be like when you do enter into the afterlife after you die — as you fully leave the earth realm. You will be able to overcome your fears or denial of dying."

Gerald felt a sense of joy about what Emma was telling him, and he did feel fortunate that he had reached the psychological development that allowed him to open himself up to his spiritual development. He realized that it was because Emma had broken up with him, in part, that allowed him to finally begin to accept that he could not measure and control rationally things he could not see.

But with this thought came the feeling of how much he missed being with her. He said to her, "Emma, does this mean we can get back together again?"

She turned serious, but then said, "No, Gerald. I've moved on in the earth realm. I am with someone else now."

He felt distressed...and felt himself beginning to float back into his consciousness lying in a meditative trance on his bed.

As he became conscious of himself breathing rhythmically in his bed, he remembered Emma saying to him as he floated away, "We will always be together in some ways...continue connecting with these spiritual dimensions...you are so much more than you and me, and you have spiritual opportunities to meet other essences of being that will enhance you while you are living in the earth realms, as well as prepare you for a peaceful transition when entering into afterlife realms.

After coming out of this visualization, Gerald realized he must still be at the beginning of developing his ability to meditate and spiritually journey into beyond life dimensions. He felt invigorated, though, from his experience entering into these dimensions and seeing Emma. He felt a sense of peacefulness that he had not felt for a long time. He felt a sense of contentment that not only had he accepted connecting with spiritual beyond life dimensions, which would allow him to prepare for a peaceful transition into the afterlife, but also that he was developing the capacities to do so. He smiled to himself as he decided he wanted to discuss with his parents what he has spiritually been experiencing.

Spiritual Visualizations — Experiencing Your Power to Transform Your Fears of Dying and Death

(You may not have fears or concerns about the process of your own dying or death, but if you do, this visualization may help you begin to transform and release these fears and concerns)

As you settle into your meditative state of peaceful being, imagine you are sitting in front of a beautiful table — dark or light wood, or any other type of table.

Visualize that an intricately carved wooden box, with designs and colors that please you, is on the table in front of you. Take a moment to savor the beauty of the container...then imagine yourself gently and sensually sliding your hand over the exterior of the wooden carved box and sense its solidness as well as its beauty...allow yourself to imagine the designs carved and painted into the wood...notice that there is a lid on the box which is closed.

Imagine yourself sitting back comfortably in your chair and continuing to breathe peacefully while keeping the image of the table and the wooden box in your mind...

Now bring into your consciousness what your fears or concerns are about dying death... allow yourself to fully experience the thoughts and emotions associated with your own dying and death...are these fears associated with pain, with what you feel might be the loss of your vitality and essence of being, with the unknown?

Then as you are experiencing these thoughts and emotions, imagine you are seeing essences of intense and dark colors representing what you are feeling and thinking about your own dying and death floating above the table...this density of essences can just be cloud-like, or what seem like dark beings floating through the air intermingling with your fears...

You are safe in your protective and centered state of being. Breathe comfortably and deeply as you watch what your fears of dying and death might look like floating above the wooden box on the table in front of you. If you begin to feel too uncomfortable know that you can open your eyes and return to your ordinary rational consciousness at any time.

When you are ready you are going to transform these dark essences into light. When you are ready imagine that you are opening the lid of box. And then imagine that you are reaching up and spreading your arms to gather the pulsating essences, compressing them, and pulling them down into the wooden box on the table, and after you do, gently close the lid.

Focus your attention on the wooden box that contains the essences of what you may be fearing about dying and death, and know that this box — as well as you — have the power of transforming these dark essences into light and spiritual love. Imagine that these essences are actually a part of the wonderment of beyond life dimensions...

Breathe deeply inhaling and exhaling rhythmically for a few moments...this transformation will not take too much time...what seemed like dark essences were just reflections of your own projections of fear, and their true essences of being have always been full of light and compassion and love and joy.

Reach forward and open the lid. Then sit back continuing to breathe rhythmically as you watch these essences, having turned back into lovely translucent essences of white light, float from the wooden box and surround you with a comforting and caressing state of being...then imagine these lovely essences dissolving away in all directions back into beyond life dimensions...

Continue to breathe deeply and savor the visions and comforting feelings of your fears transformed...and then when you are ready, allow yourself to open your eyes, and reflect on the transformation of these dark projections of your fears of dying and death into the caressing white essences of the spiritual dimensions of the afterlife.

The 12th House — Keys to Opening the Gateway to Spiritual Dimensions

I n astrology, the **Houses** represent twelve *life experiences*, its meanings derived from the phases of the cycle of the earth spinning around its axis.

The **Signs** represent twelve *natural inclinations or ways of being*, its meanings derived from the phases of the tropical zodiacal earth's cycle around the sun.

The **Planets** represent *psychological-spiritual functions* or *capacities* within the consciousness of each individual's psyche — functions that allow the individual to express one's unique natural inclinations within life experiences that are both emphasized by the moment of birth in a specific location (longitude and latitude) on earth.

The Twelfth House symbolizes life experiences related to an individual's connection and receptivity to spiritual realms. The Twelfth House is the individual's gateway into connecting with beyond life dimensions. The way an individual can open this gateway is by using a variety of special keys, or practices or awareness.

One key for opening the gateway is consciously analyzing one's dreams. Dreams are archetypal messages from the unconscious, in essence from psychological realms and spiritual dimensions. Some dreams relate to the shadows and growth potentials that are beneficial for us to be conscious of in our daily life journeys in the earth realm. Some dreams relate to beyond life dimensions and connections to the afterlife.

I believe that the growth therapies of Carl Jung are one of the most holistic approaches to analyzing dreams in terms of both psychological as well as spiritual insights. I have always felt the positive aim of analyzing dreams is to allow messages from the unconscious to enhance one's conscious understandings.

Another way of putting this is that analyzing dreams is one of the keys to unlocking the archetypal connections shared with all people on earth, as well to entering the gateway to the spiritual, beyond life dimensions.

Another key to unlocking this gateway is through meditative practices. Meditations allow one to transcend one's rational mind, one's consciousness to enable a non-rational connection to healing dimensions that can flow through one's psyche, enhancing one's mind, body and soul.

Meditative states of being can be entered through activities such as breathing, washing dishes, gardening, walking in nature, listening to music, and watching drama that touches the soul.

Spiritual visualization is another key that unlocks the gateway to beyond life dimensions. Spiritual visualizations use meditative practices at the beginning of a process of beginning journeys into imaginative and spiritual dimensions while in the earth realm.

Start with envisioning walking up to a gate, unlocking and walking through the gate, then be open to where the imaginative and spiritual journey leads you.

Another key to open the gateway to beyond life dimensions while living in the earth realm is to become immersed in creative activities. Creative activities can be artistic, such as painting, sculpting, writing, singing, dancing, crafting, photographing, videoing, filmmaking and a combination of all these various expressions as well as others. Creativity can spring from activities related to sports, cooking, administrative planning, and even scientific and technological research and discovery.

Entering the beyond life dimensions of the 12th House can also occur by leaving your earth realm home and communing with nature, whether in your garden, a park, or the wilderness of forests, streams, rivers, lakes, oceans, mountains and deserts — all reflecting natural rhythms of the earth realm that can help you connect your natural inner spiritual rhythms.

Intimacy as the Temporary Deaths of Our Egos

Each time we make love in the earth realm, we can willingly temporarily die in each other's arms for moments of exquisite intertwining of our bodies and souls. We can become intimate beyond our separate beings requiring the temporary deaths of each our egos, allowing us to attend to and satisfy each other's desires as much as our own self-oriented desires.

As we make love, we can gladly temporarily transcend parts of our egos, allowing our essences of being blending with our love partner to surround each other through the transcendental acts of intimacy, joining together our separate souls to create a rebirth of one love soul.

This act of transformative intimacy often can be our first experiences of transcending death through exquisite expressions of lovemaking... and could allow us to release the fear of our own ultimate actual deaths and transcendental resurrections as we flow into the intimate embraces of the afterlife.

Make Love With Death

Sometimes as you lie in bed before falling to sleep, imagine opening your psyche to visiting dimensions beyond your life on earth. Such a practice of traveling within your consciousness to these spiritually loving dimensions can give you peace. These meditations can enhance your daily life, connecting with spiritual dimensions and preparing you for entering into the afterlife gracefully when your time of dying arrives.

One might envision death as an exciting and spiritual lover...a lover who at some moment in your future time of dying, would be lovingly and intimately blending with your soul.

Envision death not as a dark unloving entity hovering over you to take you unwillingly away from the joys of your current life on earth, but as a lover with the aura of passionate and spiritual blends of light, a lover who will be sharing intimately the ecstasies of afterlife dimensions where spiritually romantic dreams are derived from...

Imagine at your time of dying you would be flowing into the exquisite embrace of a transcendental lover, and you will be comforted and cuddled within the caresses of other essences in the afterlife. Imagine as your soul passes from your body, your death lover would bring you into the spiritually orgasmic existence shared by the transformative passions of the many — of all essences that have ever and will ever exist. In the afterlife you will never feel abandoned and lonely, never alone.

Make Love With Death #2

A s he lay on his back, alone in his bed, dying from a lingering illness waiting for death to come take him away, he felt a spiritual darkness slide sensually over his body, his being, and his soul...

He felt at first a gentle kiss...and then a passionate kiss that seemed to reawaken his passions that he had felt he had lost. He felt the fullness of love throughout his dying body.

As a caressing darkness of love embraced him, he felt the fiery passions of intimacy in a new sparkling and embracing way.

He reached out with his soul, his whole being, and embraced his spiritual lover whom he knew would bring him into dimensions of a spiritual blending...

His lover, death, eased his pain, eased his fears, comforted him, and then showed him what it meant to experience the spiritual intimacy beyond life. He experienced a spiritual orgasm...a release from all his pain, all his fears as he joyfully entered into what he thought was the unknown, but then realized was the all-encompassing embrace of a familiar lover.

When I Die — Sweet Dreams and Memories

E ven if I am alone as I transition into the afterlife, I want to take the memories of the essences of all of you; my love, my children, my grandchildren, and my friends. I want you to know I will continue to visit all of you in your sweet dreams and dreams...don't cry for the loss of me. I remain and will be there always for all of you...

When I Die — Soul Cuddling

I want to continue to visit my loved ones still living in the earth realm and to cuddle them in their day and night dreams as they sleep, and beyond their dreams as they might need encouraging hugs during challenging times and as celebrating embraces during joyful times.

As the Ninety-Year-Old Woman Dies

A ninety-year-old woman lay in the hospital hospice bed feeling what she referred to in a joking manner as being in exquisite pain...she had not wanted medication because she wanted to remain aware of her loved ones and her nurses and caretakers as long as she could, until she passed... She knew they were giving her some medications to keep her pain bearable, yet she was appreciative that she had remained cognizant enough to interact with family and friends and medical staff.

At times she wondered what was taking so long for the moment of passing to come, and it wasn't because she wanted to leave the pain she was feeling, or her family she loved. She just felt that her moment of passing was near, and she had been spiritually preparing for this moment through her whole life.

She had been born a Catholic, but left that religion at a young age, and then continued to explore her spiritual path until she recognized that all religions were the same, all were trying to achieve the same spiritual connections. She then began practicing the meditations and personal rituals that had allowed her to connect with the spiritual world. She had visited India and studied in an ashram. She had spent time learning shamanic rituals. She had studied the Tibetan Book of the Dead and other books through the years. She felt that in her mediations, rituals and even dreams, she had entered into beyond life dimensions often. She felt no fear...and now that she knew she was dying would even say to whoever was around her in a mock irritated voice... "What is taking so long...?"

She had been alone during the morning of the day she died, but then her 18-year-old great-grandson came to sit by her bedside. He reached out to hold her hand as he talked with her. She had always felt a close bond with him, and was happy she had lived long enough to see him grow into a caring young man. He was telling her about memories of singing and dancing with her over the years. She had given him a crystal that he wore on a thin chain around his neck, and he said this gave him joy and peace. She felt happy to recognize a spiritual essence coming from him even at his young age. And as he held her hand, and as they looked into each other's eyes, she knew it was time. She had difficulty talking, but she told her great-grandson that she was so happy he was here with her, and to not feel sad but to remember her with joy, and she would be with him always.

Then she closed her eyes in peace, smiling as she experienced that time of transcending had finally come…

Amazing Journeys Into Beyond Life Dimensions

We may not know for sure what's coming next after we die, but many who are open to spiritual dimensions have had visions and dreams and have been receptive to connections from beyond life dimensions. Some people who live only through the filters of their rationality may deny the existence of the afterlife, but why not honor those who have developed their faculties of seeing beyond our ordinary minds?

For centuries most people have lived their lives tied to a small area of their locations, and in tribes and never knew the world at large. It is interesting that some people in our current society, who use their computers and phones to connect with others throughout the world beyond space and time, still deny that we can connect with vast other dimensions and realities with our own inner psychic natures.

While we are living on our earth, we can take amazing journeys into beyond life dimensions...and not only prepare ourselves for our final end-of-life journey, but we can also be experiencing these journeys while we are living, just as when we travel, while living in the earth realm, to other places both on and beyond earth. Let's imagine the best of possibilities for our end-of-life journey.

If we can develop the ability to travel to these other dimensions beyond our earth realm, we will be able to bring back transcendental treasures, visions and insights to enhance our daily lives as we continue to spiritually evolve. Being receptive to beyond life dimensions is not only spiritually beneficial to each of us, but also beneficial to others and the world. We will be exploring the spiritual dimensions of transcendental inspiration that flows through all of us and all the dimensions of existence, enriching and nourishing our souls as we take amazing journeys while we are living and after we transcend.

The Sparks of Life, the Fires of the Afterlife

You will experience the spiritual love of being, as the sparks of life float into the illuminating fires and enduring warmth of the afterlife.

As the sparks of your consciousness flow away from your earth body, your soul will become holistically balanced with earth, air and water...and the higher energy of fire's combination of lighted awareness as the dynamics of transformative energy continues to fuel transcendental evolution.

When your soul leaves the sparks of life in the earth realm, it will burst into the fires of the afterlife lighting the way as you travel through infinite dimensions of being, experiencing and developing different sides of your spiritual potentials. As your journey transcends beyond the limits of the Sun that has sustained the sparks of your life in the earth realm, your soul will burn brighter and brighter with the fires of spiritual energy that transcends all the stars of the galaxies we could ever imagine...

Crossing the Universe

I imagine that when I die, my being will transform into a space pod the shape of a an intensely hued blue and golden winged butterfly that will allow me to transcend the galaxies within and beyond my dreams, my limitations of being, and take me to unknown destinations, visiting other souls on similar journeys to find new forms of being, further expressions and evolution of our consciousness and spirituality.

I can imagine traveling beyond the speed of darkness (WHICH ON EARTH IS MEASURED STILL BY THE SPEED OF LIGHT) to visit planets and galaxies that may not exist any longer in physical forms, but that will allow my soul to dissolve within the light of stars as I continue to evolve and transcend into dimensions beyond my imagination.

When I Die — I Want to Visit the Spirits of the Planets

As my essence floats away from this precious earth, I would first like my soul to travel a ways out to visit the expansive essence of Jupiter to gain the kind of celestial understandings and overview that will give me spiritual awareness on my new journey.

Then I would like to flow back toward the **Sun** to visit *Venus* to express my appreciation for the aesthetics and sensuality of the beauty, love, social harmony and connections I have experienced in my life, which I will certainly miss as I leave the earth realm...though, I expect to be able to experience these qualities in even more interactive ways as I blend with the essences of beyond life dimensions.

Then before I head away from the **Sun's** center of this shining galaxy. I will visit and chat with *Mercury* a bit — if I can get a word in edgewise — but I want to express my appreciation for the help I received to develop my rational mind...or else how would I be able to analyze, synthesize and communicate all the non-rational, transcendental, poetic insights and visions my psyche received as I dreamed during the night and at times during the day. *Jupiter* already provided me with an understanding and an overview of life and the afterlife, but I know **Mercury** has helped me fill in the details to be able to communicate fully with all the other essences I will meet in the afterlife...

Before I begin my journey back out, I will thank the *Sun* for helping me development my unique consciousness, the center of my being and giving me the confidence to develop my special life purposes.

Then as I flow away from the Sun and **Mercury**, I will throw a kiss to *Mother Earth* as I pass by, and will treasure all the life sustaining support and sensual opportunities she has provided me through my life in her realm.

As I begin my journey back out to the further planets of the galaxy, I will playfully tussle and spar with *Mars*, hoping his spirit is in a good mood...knowing that my journey and spiritual purpose will be energized from my contact with this planet's essence.

I will float slowly past the feminine **asteroids** and again experience the interactive, equal receptivity and wisdom they have and will continue to provide me as I continue my spiritual journey and transition.

As I pass by Jupiter again, I will share the image and essence of a flower that **Venus** planted within my soul.

When I reach *Saturn*, I look forward to receiving amazing constructive guidance, and I will have prepared for his judgments and challenges, knowing this ringed planet means well in helping to set meaningful boundaries. I will welcome and treasure any lessons provided to me as I transition into deeper spiritual levels of maturity.

I then will visit with **Chiron** and hope any wounds I may still carry within my soul will be healed through this special contact.

As I flow further out into transcendental, transpersonal realms, I will visit **Uranus**, who has allowed me and others on earth to experience the collective spiritual insights that have come from all diverse essences of being existing in the earth realms and beyond life dimensions. With this visit, I will look forward to fully embracing my creative mental powers to connect with others, both in this realm I'm leaving, and all other dimensions. **Uranus** will help me see the infinite possibilities of the future beyond space and time as I enter into afterlife dimensions.

Next, I will visit visionary, empathetic, compassionate *Neptune* where all dreams, poetic imagery, and musical artistic expressions come from, and where the spiritual, unconscious mysteries within our psyches reside. **Neptune's** spirit will allow me to merge with the essences of all beings. I hope I'll be able to stay for a while immersed in the exquisite seas of the unknown before I continue my journey.

My last visit will be to *Pluto*, where the power and purpose of my soul will be elevated beyond the galaxy of planets. **Pluto's** visit will enhance my power of spiritual transformation, allowing me to leave the physical realms of the solar system that have provided me and all life forms on earth and other planets to exist and develop within cycles of being and becoming.

And then...then...I will travel through other galaxies until I float away into the afterlife with the treasures of being that I have been fortunate enough to receive during my cosmic journey.

Reaching Beyond the Stars

Reaching out beyond our minds and our visions we first allow the stars to inspire us, twinkling within our souls...

We can also allow our psyches to reach beyond the stars in our inner envisioning...to not only enjoy, but to be spiritually enhanced...

Our spiritual visions can be infinitely expansive...but often limited by our rational minds not being open to dimensions beyond cognition and by our conditioning...

Let's develop the meditative capacities to travel to the stars and beyond within our psychic visions and bring back into daily lives transcendental inspirations...

Episodes From TV Shows That Dramatize Aspects of Death & Dying

"Star Trek: The Next Generation"

Season 1, Episode 22 — The security officer Lieutenant Tasha Yar dies, but she left a holographic video of her saying goodbye to all the other crew members. It was quite emotional and uplifting when it was played at her memorial ceremony. It made me think of how leaving words of love and caring before dying would be a special way of saying goodbye as well as helping to heal those left beyond.

Season 31, Episode 16 — Data, the android, creates a humanoid android based upon his own structural design and advanced skills in cybernetics. He describes the android as his child, and gives it a female appearance, and names her Lal (after Hindi world for "beloved"). With the help of Troi, the crew's counselor, he tries to teach her how to relate to humans and attempts to develop her cognitive skills. She progresses at a fast pace, but suddenly her circuitry fails, and she dies. Before she dies, she is able to convey her love to Data as her father. Later Captain Picard expresses condolences, but Data reveals that he has downloaded Lal's memories into his own neural net, allowing Lal's memories, experiences and being to live on completely within his own mind. As humans, we are capable of keeping the memories and essences of being of the loved ones we have lost in the spiritual beyond database of our psyches.

"Bones"

Season 6, Episode 9 — Temperance Brennan (Bones) is a forensic scientist, who assists the FBI in analyzing bones in order to identify victims as well as determine the specific time and causes of the victim's death. Bones is a highly rational person who does not believe in religion or aspects of life that is not evidence-based.

In this episode, Bones is evaluating a female victim who was a brilliant and career-driven woman, just like Bones herself. This victim died with no family or romantic connections. Bones discovered that the victim also had a similar childhood as she had. Bones' parents abandoned her and her brother and she spent years in foster care. While Bones enjoys sexual relationships, she is resistant to falling in love. When Bones listens to an audio recording of the woman, her voice reminds her of her own voice, and she begins to compare her own life with the life of the victim, who stated in the video that she had regrets of not taking advantage of love opportunities. Throughout the episode, Bones is forced to think about her own approach to love, and about life and death and what her spiritual beliefs are. This episode dramatizes the benefits of continuing to seek to overcome past traumas and blind spots so that we can live fully with love and develop a spiritual attunement to life and death.

Season 8, Episode 9 — The bones of a young boy are brought into the Jefferson Forensic Lab for evaluation in an attempt to determine how the body died or was killed. Throughout the episode each of the staff separately comes to the bones, and while the scene is being shot from the angle of the boy, each staff member talks to the boy as if his spirit could understand and communicate with them. It is a powerful episode conveying connection with afterlife beyond rational science.

These are just a few examples of creative expressions, and I know there are many more in literature, music, paintings and other visual art, movies, and theater that can expand our awareness and visions about death and the afterlife. We can use these creative, artistic and dramatic expressions to help us grow through cathartic and inspirational experiences.

"Alexa, Repeat My Life"

And Alexa responded, "Sorry, I don't know how to do that. But here's something you might try...You can ask me what your favorite musical choices are? You can ask me to tell you a bedtime story...You can also ask me to tell you a joke."

I knew what Wily Wizard would ask, but I said, as gently as I could, "Alexa, stop."

Then I thought, "Do I really want to repeat all my life experiences? I mean, some of them I certainly would like to re-experience, but not everything...maybe I could make a psychic playlist of my special memories, and then I wouldn't mind it if Alexa would take me back to the past to re-experience these special times...

Maybe one day our collective consciousness will be able to relive meaningful experiences of the past in real time — whatever that means — and remember who we are in whatever future dimension we are existing in — with the wisdom and knowledge gained though time and beyond time...and perhaps we would be able to explore making different choices in different timelines...but maybe I wouldn't change anything. I'm satisfied with the memories that remain in my mind and with the photos and memorabilia of the past.

When I Die — The Essences of Being I'd Like to Get Together With

I would first like to get together with Dane Rudhyar, Carl Jung and Rumi to discuss the array of spiritual and psychological archetypes they identified and envisioned...

I would like to get together with F. Buckminster Fuller and discuss with him how much he enjoyed expanding into infinite dimensions...

I'd like to get together with Maya Angelou, Emily Dickinson, Jane Austin, Toni Morrison, Virginia Wolfe and enjoy their creative passion and insights...

I'd like to get together with Anais Nin, Henry Miller, Lawrence Durrell and Gertrude Stein and hear about the creative adventures and wild liberations of the 20s and 30s in Paris...

I'd like to get together with Lawrence Ferlinghetti, Ken Kesey, Jack Kerouac, and ok...Timothy Leary and even Hunter Thompson to see if they enjoy spiritually getting high...

I'd like to get together with Martin Luther King, John Lewis, Harriot Tubman and George Floyd among many others to see how they might be influencing the evolving racial and income equality movements not just in the US, the rest of the earth, but also in other physical realms...

I'd like to get together with Buddha, Allah, Yahweh, Jesus and Mary, Rumi, Kahlil Gibran, Ram Dass and have a discussion of spiritual unity and joy...

I'd like to get together with Jane Roberts and Seth if they are around. I'd like to find out if they really stopped reincarnating, and to see if they are mentors now. I'd be curious to see what realities and dimensions they have been creating for themselves. I wonder if they are mentors and if so, do they get together with Wily Wizard from time to time or rather beyond time to anytime — and share spiritual wisdom and laughter...

I'd like to get together with David Bowie, Edith Piaf, Leonard Cohen, Whitney Houston, Luciano Pavarotti, Billie Holiday, Mozart, Janis Joplin and Amy Winehouse — and I don't mind being considered an afterlife groupie...I would like to hear their new music...

I know that I will be happy to be getting together again with my loved ones and friends, as well as new essences I will meet and blend with...it can also be meaningful to imagine getting together with individuals representing the evolutional ideas and expressions to expand our own growth while living in this earth realm.

Who would you like to meet and visit with if you could journey into beyond life dimensions before you die, or when you finally do transition into the afterlife?

Spiritual Joy

J oy...we feel joy when we hold our lover, as we hold our children, as we experience the accomplishments and recognitions of who we are and who we have become. Different ones of us feel joy as we ride the rapids of a river in nature; as we jump out of an airplane as a skydiver (that's not something I would enjoy — I would be traumatized for sure); as we make love and have a loving and intimate, interdependent orgasm (Now, I can relate to that! Can't you?).

But what is spiritual joy...it's connecting with something beyond river rapids, jumping out of an airplane, even...ok, maybe even having a physical and emotional orgasm (even though I think that can, of course, be quite spiritual also).

Spiritual joy is opening one's psyche, one's being to a dimension that can provide us joys beyond what we could ever experience on earth, in our earth bodies.

Adjectives are meant to expand the meanings of a noun — and a state of being...yes, let's not just expand our consciousness, let's transcend the limitations of joys, in spiritual dimensions, while we are living and when we transcend into the afterlife with spiritual joy.

Embrace this transcendental descriptive adjective meaning of the word spiritual. If there are joys we can experience beyond our mundane sweet earth realm existences...let's embrace those joys.

What Does Spirituality Mean?

W hat does spirituality mean? How is spirituality different from religion?

How can you become spiritual? Take a deep breath, meditate, play your most inspiring spiritual music (or, if you are so inclined, religious music which might also allow your soul to connect to beyond life dimensions as you transcend religious doctrines).

Spirituality is the capacity within your psyche and consciousness that allows the core essence of yourself to be able to blend with everything else in existence. Spiritually is being individually one beyond one at the same time

We can learn from spiritual guides from this earth realm and from beyond life dimensions, but these guides are not gods or goddesses or beyond gender gods and goddesses (maybe androgynous...). Wily Wizard would even agree. Anyway, these spiritual guides just have some information that may help you in your own journeys...like going to an acupuncturist, or a surgeon...they don't try to control everything you do or don't do...they try to provide healing service or guidance to allow you to heal yourself...to allow you to reach the spiritual potentials within yourself. You are the channel for the expression of spiritual realities...you are the essence of what some people refer to as Gods with omnipotent powers. You have all the powers within yourself. We each do.

Spirituality is not limited to a one and only god...not limited to higher beings who control and judge your every behavior. Spirituality means the direct connection to all that exists in beyond life dimensions...it is beyond the belief systems of the Christian,

Judaic or Islamic beliefs in heaven or hell...spirituality is the nurturing and accepting essence of existences in our earth life realms and in all other beyond life dimensions.

We can connect and receive this nurturing and unconditional life if we open our psyches to transcendental spiritual dimensions beyond the distortions of especially monolithic religions.

Wily Wizard's Unreality Show — Episode #1:

Competitive discussions between advocates for religious, spiritual, and non-religious visions of the afterlife

Religious Advocate: History has shown that people need a religious leader to define who the one and only God is, and also the practices that will allow them to transition into Heaven or Hell...whatever the higher and lower places of eternity are as defined by the doctrines of the religion.

Spiritual Advocate: These doctrines of the various religions seem to be aimed at controlling behavior of people while they are living — and these controlled behaviors seem mostly for the benefit of those humans who developed and are currently advocating the doctrines and dogma as the right path to achieving some special place in the afterlife. I believe that individuals can connect directly with spiritual dimensions while living and as they transition into the afterlife. I do believe that the various rituals of prayer, singing, collective sharing and so on — all can allow a person to connect to the spiritual realms...

Non-Religious Advocate (Shaking her head): Religion...Spirituality...I don't believe in any of those foolish, non-evidence-based illusions. The afterlife is a fanciful belief that is meant to keep people docile and hopeful that life will get better after they die, or that they will continue to enjoy whatever privilege they've achieved (often at the expense or the well-being of others) after they die.

Religious Advocate (also shaking his head): How did she get in here?

Spiritual advocate (holding up her hands): Let's be inclusive here...Let's see what we can define that can bring us together...

Religious Advocate: I'm not used to that. Most religions only want to save those who believe in their Gods — one and only God...

Non-Religious Advocate: Science has not proven there is an afterlife...so what's there to agree to if both of you believe there is...

Spiritual Advocate: But science has not disproven the existence of the afterlife either.

Non-Religious Advocate: How can you prove something that doesn't exist...

Spiritual Advocate: Even if you can't prove that spiritual and afterlife dimensions exist, do you deny that meditation, love for all peoples and other life forms can help make people's lives more enriching and caring? I'm just trying to find something we can agree on — though of course I do believe spiritual dimensions both in a person's life on earth and in the afterlife do exist.

Religious Advocate: Only if you choose a one and only God to pledge allegiance to — or what's the point of religion?

Non-Religious Advocate: There is no point in believing in something you can't scientifically prove...that gods or goddesses or the afterlife exist...

Spiritual Advocate: Oh come on...there is plenty of evidence that dimensions beyond our rational awareness, and that scientific instruments can measure do exist...

At this point, all three of the contestants seemed to have reached an impasse, and then all three turned to Wily Wizard, who was supposed to be moderating the competitive discussion.

Wily Wizard seemed to be dozing instead of paying attending to the discussion.

The Non-Religious Advocate: Wily Wizard! I can't believe you are sleeping!

Wily Wizard opened his eyes: Aha! You made an assumption you cannot prove...I may have been dozing, but I was carefully listening to all that you were talking about from my dream world, or what some may call a beyond life dimension...This disqualifies you because your lack of evidence-based assumption undermines your beliefs. You can leave now.

Wily Wizard turned to the Religious and Spiritual Advocates: You two have reached the finals of this obviously unreal competition. This final phase will not occur until each of you come into your next lifetimes. If only one of you make it, then of course she is the winner. If both of you make it, then whoever has the most dramatic and non-boring story of how you made it into the afterlife will win.

Wily Wizard turned to the Religious Advocate: I suggest you choose a religion that believes in reincarnation if you want to win this totally unreal competition. You can leave now...

After the Religious Advocate left Wily Wizard then turned to the Spiritual Advocate: I don't know why I agreed to moderate this discussion because I already know who the winner is, but when I see you in the next lifetime, I will still expect you to tell me a good joke or I may just disqualify you anyway...the potentials for laughter based on nonsensical spiritual evolvement is how I decide to choose who are the winners of these ridiculous unreal reality shows are...though I'm not saying that's the only criteria...just the most delightful criteria...if you believe in the spiritual pathway of laughter.

Excerpts From a Journal of a Neophyte Seeker
Exploring Religious and Non-Religious Visions of the
Afterlife

I was not raised in a religious family, so I never learned any religious doctrine in depth. Yet recently I've become obsessed with seeking the right pathway that will lead me to a positive existence in the afterlife. I decided to explore various religious pathways that may lead to the afterlife. I'll document my search in the following journal entries. As I review my thoughts and feelings I've written during my explorations I realize that I may not have always understood the full meanings of the doctrines and practices of these religions I tried to explore and at least temporarily immerse myself in...but I did the best I could and I'm only at the beginning of this spiritual search, and besides, nobody is supposed to read this journal anyway except you, so I can make mistakes in how I understand some things...though I have to admit that if I think that one of these omnipotent gods or goddesses do exist they will know what I'm writing in my journal anyway — but I'm willing to take that spiritual risk of upsetting some higher being if I haven't understood some doctrine in the right way. Whoever that so called-higher being is shouldn't be reading my private journal anyway without my permission. Though I guess if this higher being is omnipotent then they would just know what I've written. I can't worry about everything — I just want to continue my search...

Exploring the Christian vision of the afterlife...

As I explored this vision of the afterlife, I read passages from the Bible and prayed every day as I awoke and before I went to sleep. I have an icon of Mary Magdalene on the cabinet of my bedroom. I try to feel connected to "Jesus our Lord", because he died for my sins, whatever they are. I'm not trying to be sacrilegious. I know I'm not perfect. I guess I have to study the Ten Commandments and the...so called New Testaments to make sure I know what Jesus is covering for me, my sins. I'm not trying to be sacrilegious, oh god, no. I'm new at this and I'm trying to make a good faith effort to try to prepare for the afterlife. I've started exploring the Christian viewpoint, pathway, expectations, judgment demands...and I will try to do my best. I know that judgment is part of all these religions but so is forgiveness, right? Anyway I will be trying to explore to prepare for entering into the afterlife in the best way I can...ok, I admit...I do want to avoid being sent to Hell, if it turns out the Christian religion is the right one.

Some people may think I'm just trying to hedge my bets so to speak...just trying to make sure I try to appease all religions so maybe one will forgive me for spreading myself out. I know this is a losing proposition because most of these religions have, as a premise, that theirs is the only one, and so maybe one day before I die, I will have to choose...I'll see about that. I'm just at the beginning of my religious preparation for exploring to be embraced by the Christian God when I enter the afterlife.

I think I understand that Christians do believe that human existence does not end at physical death. I agree with that. But I can become anxious about their beliefs that the consequences of whatever sin I have committed will follow me there, and I will be judged and maybe sent to purgatory where maybe, I can eventually be cleansed, or Hell, if there is no Christian hope for redemption for me. Oh my gosh (I hope He notices I didn't write, "Oh My God", but maybe I should have written OMG! and then let Him choose what "G" stands for as He wishes...of course he knows anyway...I guess).

In my preparation for transcending into the graces of the Christian God in the afterlife, I pray every day. I sit comfortably and do just like the monks of the Middle Ages and in modern times still do. I repeat words, such as "Godly Light", "Godly love", "Peace", and allow my rational thoughts to disintegrate into the spiritual dimensions that we are all trying to connect our souls with.

I will keep the symbolism of Christian transcendence around me. I'll keep a wooden cross, the symbol of where Jesus was crucified. When I enter a temple of worship, I will kneel on my right knee, sometimes both knees, but as I have gotten older, it's a little harder to stand back up, and I hope God will forgive me for that. Since he or she or beyond gender doesn't age, I guess, I just hope He, She, ??...has empathy. Should, right? Oh, I also have a symbol of a fish because somewhere I read that this relates to Jesus, but also, I am in love with a Pisces woman, not that I believe in astrology...oh God no...Have mercy on me...

I want to emphasize again on my behalf, that I also sit in front of a visual representation of the cross, and of Jesus, and of Mary Magdalene — I have to admit I spend more time looking at Mary Magdalene than Jesus — not just because she is a woman, oh gosh no! But she may be the wisest person of Christian lore. I just adore her...her spiritual essence, that is, it seems to me she transcends the patriarchal scriptures. But what do I know?

OK, I'm not doing well here while preparing for the Christian potentials of the afterlife. I will move on to the next religion, but...I do love you, Jesus and God and the Trinity and especially Mary...have mercy on my soul, and at least just send me to purgatory if you don't think I'm right for Heaven yet. I think I can be cleansed. I'd like the opportunity for that...at least if the water is a bit warm, and not too hot.

Before I religiously move on, I want to acknowledge that Christian art often depicts Jesus as symbolizing the first and last letters of the Greek alphabet, Alpha and Omega, and is supposed to represent the beginning and the end of all things. The end of all things? Does that mean the end of all human things, all life forms, all spiritual things, all things that we don't even know about? I never think of existence ending, but transitioning, transforming, expanding...anyway, on to my next attempt at preparing for the afterlife...

Exploring the Catholic vision of the afterlife...

I decided that while I'm in this Christian state of religious exploration, I should look at a few offshoots of these doctrines...maybe one of these can help me better prepare and enter into the afterlife realm on more acceptable terms.

It seems like there is not really much difference between the Catholic religious view of the afterlife than other Christian offshoots. Except that Catholic dogma seem much more elitist, and that salvation in the afterlife only is bestowed on those who have long believed in their religious doctrines. Yet, I understand that modern Catholics are much more open to forgiveness and atonement for those who do not believe in their religious doctrines...which will give me some peace of mind if I ultimately choose this pathway.

In my preparation for the Catholic transition into the afterlife, I love to sit in cathedrals around the world, those beautiful buildings that were built on the backs of common laborers who often died for lack of nutrition or health care...but these buildings are both intricately and expansively inspirational, and the music...oh, the music in the cathedrals...emotionally uplifting... as well as the beauty of the stained-glass depictions of the saints and wonderment of life and the afterlife... I have enjoyed visiting these cathedrals, and have found myself transported into a spiritual place...which leaves me to believe that spiritual attunement transcends religious transgressions and monotheistic doctrines. I do believe that all religions have some elements of true spirituality at their core. Maybe all were derived from true spiritual connections.

Exploring the Protestant vision of the afterlife...

I have understood that the Protestants beliefs are similar in essence to all Christian beliefs, including Catholicism, but they don't believe in the Pope. They still believe in resurrection of Jesus at the end of time that will save us all...most of us. But Hell is still a possibility, and is a place of eternal torment, even though I have understood that some modern Protestants do not feel that it is consistent with a loving god. I'm with them...these modern Protestants...who wouldn't be?

I realize my attempt to make sure I determine the best religion or spiritual pathway that may help me enter the afterworld unscathed and, in a way, leading to a heavenly existence and certainly not in an underworld way of eternal pain and suffering...even writing that makes me feel anxious...but this attempt I'm making may seem a bit too self-oriented. Maybe something I learn along the way will help me transcend this fear. Maybe not. Anyway, I can imagine how this prospect of going to hell in the afterlife was very convenient for those who wanted to control the population, and continue to subject them to subhuman living conditions over the centuries…

If I choose this pathway, at least I won't have to deal with a Priest as an intermediary standing between God and humans as I prepare for a positive afterlife. While I might embrace the protestant idea that the priestly vocation or calling does not have to involve the special status of a Priest, I'm not happy about the Calvinistic "work ethic" that has allowed capitalism to exploit cheap labor over the centuries. Now wait a second, why am I dealing with the misuse of religious dogma related to the work ethic to take advantage and harm workers, when I'm just trying to prepare for a wonderful transition into the afterlife using various religious dogmas and doctrines and spiritually enhancing rituals of music, sharing and compassion?

All I can say is that there is a difference between religious dogma, hypocritical applications and transcendental spiritual practices…I'm trying to sort this out…

Exploring the Judaic vision of the afterlife…

Immediately after I awake, I wash my hands and thank God for restoring my soul. And before I go to sleep, I recite the Ha-Mapil blessing imploring God to grant me a peaceful sleep. These are among the many blessings I recite throughout the day as I explore the Judaic vision of the afterlife.

In my spiritual search I came across something that Maimondides (1135-1205) wrote (though that was a long time ago…it may still have some controversial relevance over 800 years later): "In the world to come there is no eating, drinking, washing, anointing or sexual intercourse, but the righteous sit with their crowns on their heads enjoying the radiance of the Divine Presence.

I don't know, but even though I will miss the sensual and sexual pleasures in the afterlife, I have figured there is much more, so much more than just sitting with a crown on my head enjoying the radiance of the Divine Presence. Is everyone else able to have crowns and enjoy the Divine Presence, or will I be a privileged elite being enjoying the presence of the Jewish God while other essences toil in Hell or somewhere in between? I have to spiritually reconcile this...

And then I have understood that the Jewish God has promised to make their followers a sacred people and give them a holy land. I cannot accept this if it is at the expense of peoples from other religions. I'm not trying to just be hard on Judaism — forgive me if I seem that way...but all of these first religions I am exploring are so tribal, demanding that their spiritual pathway is the only true pathway to transcending to the higher, more positive realms of the afterlife. I'm not sure if I can follow such narrow and non-inclusive pathways.

I think I understand that there are four main movements within Judaism, so I'm kind of stymied. If I attempt to follow this religious pathway into the afterlife, which is the right pathway? And I'm only dealing with one dogma/doctrine here! I just have to keep searching for the right religious pathway that may blend with what I consider an inclusive, spiritual pathway.

Exploring the Islamic vision of the afterlife...

According to the Prophet Muhammad I will need to surrender or submit to the will of Allah, the creator of the world. According to the Quran, Islam believes that Allah is the one true God with no equal. While there are differences between the Sunni and Shi'a division within Islam, both seem to require followers to adhere to the Five Pillars of Islam in order to be acceptable to Allah. As I prepare for obtaining the Islam transition into the higher realms of the afterlife, I know I will need to observe these Five Pillars of Islam:

Shahada — I will pledge my faith;
Salat — I will practice ritual prayer;
Zadat — I provide charity to the poor;
Sawm — I will fast during the month of Ramadan;
Hajj — I will pilgrimage to the holy city of Mecca.

Oh, and I have to acknowledge that "There is no god but God (Allah), and Muhammad is the messenger of God." Just as the Gods of the various sects of Christianity and Judaism want me to swear to...I'll have to carefully and spiritually try to figure this out so I don't follow the wrong path to my salvation (if that's the right word) in the afterlife. I'm even getting more anxious here about making the wrong choice...

But I do believe the ritual practices might be helpful in connecting to the spiritual dimensions such as praying in the direction of Mecca (though I guess for me prayer is like meditating and why couldn't I make spiritual connections as I pray in any direction?). Other practices involve the ritual of cleansing both the mind and body and the practice of charity — these are positive spiritual practices. All of the monotheistic religions I have so far explored have such spiritually attuned rituals and practices that I'm sure can help one to connect to the beyond life realms. It's just these political, man-made, tribal doctrines and dogmas seem to be rather confusing to me as I stand before the crossroads of pathways that will lead me into the spiritual realms of the afterlife.

Exploring the Hindu view of the afterlife...

As I began my exploration of the afterlife pathway of Hinduism, I realized that there are many sects and doctrines being practiced. Of course, that's a challenge for someone like me, who sometimes has a difficult time making decisions...I still wonder what pathway will allow me to achieve my goal of entering into positive spiritual dimensions of the afterlife.

What first resonated with me was the Hindu doctrine of *samsara* (the cycle of rebirth). The doctrine of karma (the universal law of cause and effect) is also related to the cycle of rebirth. Hinduism seems to have a religious goal of dissolving into the ultimate spiritual essence of Brahman after the individual has accepted the true nature of self...in which the "self" ceases to exist...and at that religious point, one stops grasping to exist, and moves outside the cycle of rebirth.

I'll put that issue aside for now about whether or not I believe in the ultimate dissolving of my consciousness. Here's what I am attracted to if I decide to follow this pathway to the afterlife — I like all these goddesses, I mean gods and goddesses (devas) that I could connect with as I continue my spiritual journey...the god, Shiva, the god, Vashnu, the goddess, Shakta, and Smarta (some essence that is beyond gods and goddesses and is spiritually connected with Brahman). I also have always liked the spiritual greeting of

Namaste. And I have liked the multitudes of colorful and spiritual shrines that exist in this religion.

I also like the religious act of puja, which involves sharing the selfless expression of love and also involves the sharing of food for the gods and goddesses...though there is something about this which could be a little disconcerting...when the family who has made the food can also partake of the food, it like as humans they are eating the left overs...though sometimes leftovers have the best taste.

But maybe this kind of hierarchical spiritual elitism is no longer practiced in today's modern world.

I haven't made my decision yet, but I will move on...I do appreciate all of the spiritual rituals of all these religions I am exploring. I know many of these practices have and will continue to allow me to connect to beyond life dimensions while I am living and then should lead me somewhere into the afterlife when I die, yet I'm just having a difficult time seeing past the shadows of human doctrines in order to see the embracing light of the afterlife...

Exploring the Buddhist vision of the afterlife...

I have understood that Buddhism was initially a way to help alleviate the suffering of the world, but now incorporates the concept of salvation, referred to as nirvana. Nirvana represents the end of rebirth. So there is another goal here related to end of individual consciousness being achieved by obtaining a higher selfless consciousness...just like those who believe in Hinduism.

Both Hinduism and Buddhism have provided those of us in the western world special meditative spiritual rituals and practices.

As I explored Buddhism in my search for ways to prepare for entering into the afterlife after I die, I became particularly attracted (I guess that's not the best concept to use with the detachment focus related to Buddhism — so I could write, I particularly appreciated in a spiritual sense unconnected to my emotions). I became particularly appreciative of the notion of the Wheel of Dharma, which I have come to understand as the potential for our individual evolution of consciousness and positive spiritual action in our current incarnation to erase our past karma.

Perhaps as we transcend into the afterlife, we will be healed anyway... not with human created gods and goddesses, no matter how exotic that may seem, but with the caring love from all essences of being who are not hierarchal gods or goddesses...with the blend of these polarities of expressions of being.

Exploring the pagan vision of the afterlife...

Fire-Earth-Air-Water — The spirituality of the natural cycles of earth as embodying the beyond life dimensions without human interference related to egotistical, power grabbing doctrines and dogmas...

I understand that some pagans believe in reincarnation, but not as sometimes relegated to some sort of prison, but rather as a process of growth and evolving into higher consciousness, and maybe as a choice.

I have understood that some pagans believe in The Summerland, a paradise of sensual pleasure, a place between reincarnations to rest and renew one's soul and I guess enjoy some physical pleasures, until the next rebirth.

Many Pagans believe that individuals can form their own viewpoints of the afterlife. Of course, I like that. I've been sludging through all these different monolithic religions and haven't felt I've been prepared in the way that makes me feel good. I want to emphasize again and again that from my perspective, all these religions I've been exploring seem to have rituals and practices that do help individuals connect to the beyond life spiritual dimensions — meditative prayers, songs, pilgrimages, living a kind and caring life without hypocrisy, (even though most religions don't really define what hypocrisy means so followers seem to be given a pass if they advocate practices that are harmful to others, but enhance their own power and wealth). I'm against some of their gods having a special place in the afterlife...I'm beginning to resist believing that any of these gods are more special than other essences of being.

Anyway, getting back to this pagan preparation for the afterlife...Pagans are focused, it seems, on embracing the spiritual in the natural world and allowing an individual to transcend peaceful and spiritually to a garden paradise in the afterlife.

Pagans seem to have an inclusive view of spiritual practices, involving setting up shrines that reflect spiritual devotion, and that includes gods and goddess from various religions, and symbols of nature...pagans use objects from the natural world such as crystals, various stones, seashells, feathers, and natural incense. These shrines provide a focal point for personal meditational practices — pagans like to create a magical and mythical essence to their personal space through collecting natural objects and special creative art...

Pagans embrace visualizations as prayer...meditative states of consciousness as a way of connecting with beyond life dimensions, and preparing for the afterlife.

The pagan path has been demonized by the Christian elite...but also by many modern scientific practitioners...many who do not recognize the spiritual world anyway...

...but I find pagan practices spiritually helpful in using positive connections with nature as gateways to becoming open to beyond life and eventually preparing for entering peacefully into afterlife dimensions."

Exploring the shamanic view of the afterlife...

I realize that what westerners refer to as shamanic beliefs and practices have been developed by various indigenous tribes throughout the world for centuries. The term *Shaman* derives from the Tungus of Siberia, and means "he who knows." There are also female shamans. Shamans use their connections with the spirit world to heal people's physical, emotional, and psychological problems and conflicts. Shamanic spiritual healers and mediums are called different names in different indigenous and Native American tribes throughout the world and the U.S.

In researching and consulting various westerner healers who have adopted and attempted to use shamanic practices, I have identified some common beliefs that I resonate with. These modern shamanic healers provide the practitioner guidance in learning techniques and rituals that will allow them to become their own spiritual medium and healer, entering into beyond life afterlife dimensions on their own without the need of a shamanic guide, even though it is believed that connective rituals with others who are on similar spiritual paths can always be beneficial.

I see a connection between some of the spiritual practices and rituals of paganism and western shamanism, especially with their uses of natural world places and objects in their rituals aimed at opening gateways into the spirit world. Shamanic rituals use places in nature, such as mountains, forests and rivers, and natural healing objects such as herbs, flowers, incense, leaves, sand, and mud to assist in connecting with spiritual dimensions.

The shamanic pathway involves taking inner journeys while in this life...as a form of meditation, as a form of conscious visualization, sometimes willingly entering into a trance and out of body experience, allowing the individual to experience spiritual joys, ecstasies and guidance through connections with beyond life dimensions.

One of the rituals involve meditatively experiencing the spiritual inner cycles of death and rebirth, where the individual consciously enters into what has been referred to as inner ego-liquefying, symbolic death processes and ceremonies. This ritual requires the individual to be able to open one's psyche to spiritual dimensions as a preparation for dying in peaceful, liberating and trusting ways.

Preparing for the atheist ideas about the afterlife...

I know that the atheist believes there is no afterlife. The atheist might say, "When I die, my consciousness, just like the flame of a candle, is blown out..." But wait a second, a candle can be relit and even if the candle burns all the way down, a new candle can be placed in the holder and relit.

This viewpoint denying there is an afterlife is like a cosmic shrug, as if the atheist is saying, "I'm here — then I'm gone — I hope you have good memories of me. I've left all my digitized photos and even texts that everyone has ever sent to me so you can remember me."

I can imagine for the more developed and compassionate atheist this viewpoint would include that people need to live good lives since that's all there is — but all religious, metaphysical, and philosophical viewpoints want us to live good and caring lives — it's just if we think there is nothing else beyond our breath and consciousness in our lifespan. It's like saying, "I don't know what tomorrow will bring so I'll truly live in the moment and do the best I can in the moment." That's not bad — no matter what I come to believe about the afterlife, I want to keep attempting to live fully in the present more and do the most caring thing we can in the present. I just happen to believe that there is something else that exists beyond the present moment and lifespan here on this earth, and I don't mind reflecting, fantasizing, envisioning, imagining—

however you want to describe these spiritual beliefs—about what the afterlife might be.

Exploring the agnostic ideas about the afterlife...

The agnostic might say, "I just don't know if there is a god or a religious doctrine that describes the spiritual world or even if the spiritual world exists. It's impossible to know if divine beings exist in some unknown dimensions. That's the point — it's unknown. Don't bother me...I have to get back to my animated science fiction show on my favorite streaming channel. I know that exists at least...unless there is a fiber optic cable disruption, I know what technological device to blame...most of the time...but in terms of preparing for my death I want to be more focused on putting my finances in order and getting rid of my belongings that nobody in my family would want, and also things that I may not want anyone to know about me...though I really do try to live life in caring, empathetic and compassionate ways..."

That last part is certainly something positive about most agnostic's behaviors as well as all of our behaviors no matter what religious or spiritual pathways to peacefully transition into the afterlife — I hope all of behaviors will be caring, empathetic and compassionate...

Exploring my own vision of the afterlife

I will continue to explore and hopefully soon will be able to figure out the best pathway for me. I think I'll step back now and try to figure out what spiritually makes sense to me about all these different pathways. Maybe this will help me choose...I'll use my journal to try to clarify my thoughts. I know I'm leaning toward a pathway that's spiritually holistic...not elite, not monolithic...and I believe our unique consciousness and soul goes on... and until I know the right pathway and while I live in this time-space reality, I will choose to live within my spiritual dreams of openness to new dimensions.

Wily Wizard's Unreality Show — Episode #2:

The Atheist, The Agnostic, The Deist, The Theist... and the Nectar of the Gods.

Atheist: I don't believe in the concept of there being a god. There is no god.

Agnostic: How do you know?

Atheist: How do you know I'm wrong?

Agnostic: I'm not saying you're wrong, but how do you know for sure?

Deist: Well of course the Atheist doesn't know for sure. God exists and many of us believe that we can use our reasoning and observation to recognize the natural laws that God has put in place for us and the universe. I believe that God created the universe but then left the outcomes to those living in the earth realms. He kind of moved on and is somewhat indifferent to us now. Though some of us believe that God does support worthy causes and believes in Providence.

Atheist: Again, why are you so sure that *I don't know for sure* about there not being an omnipotent God? I am using my reasoning which is all we can rely upon. I believe that the Deist and definitely the Theist are both wrong in believing there is a god.

Agnostic: Come on, Atheist, I still challenge you to explain how are you so sure both the Theist and Deist are wrong?

Theist: I hate to say this, but I'm on the side of the Deist and Agnostic for different reasons. As a Theist I believe that God created the universe, and *wants* to be involved and *is* involved in all that we humans are doing in our lives. Most of us believe in a monotheistic God, which is how the major western religions, like Christianity, Judaism, Islam, etc. came into being. But the Atheist is so sure there is no god either way. Just like the Agnostic, I wonder how the Atheist knows for sure.

Atheist: I feel I'm being ganged up on here...where are the scientists? Where are those who also want proof? I need help here...

Wily Wizard *(as he takes a sip of his nectar from the gods, or at least from the dimensions that reflect the best...of nectar from all dimensions — or at least that's where he says it's from):* This is silly. But I do enjoy these crazy egotistical, subjective asinine declarations that God does or does not exist — however, that's not the right question. God-capacities exist within every essence of being — though many earth based leaders use religion to try to co-opt the spiritual essence the god-capacity that exists within every one for their own benefits, like some politicians in the US who try to suppress the vote of those who tend to not vote for them...ok, sorry to bring that up now, although it makes sense if you are able to expand what you think makes inclusive sense...let's see, where was I...I don't know, but I like the Agnostic, which is kind of ironic isn't it? I think he has won this competition. I am leaning toward choosing Agnostic as the winner of these sorry spiritual competitors, but not because I think he/she/beyond she/it is right — it's just that the others are so definitely wrong in their rigid viewpoints. At least the Agnostic admits he is not sure...but you know, let's just gather around and drink some of this nectar with me...let's all become thoroughly spiritually inebriated, and maybe we won't need to have any more of these unreality spiritual show competitions...or if we do maybe we can call it Dancing Beyond the Stars and into the Afterlife.

The Neophyte Seeker's Attempt to Finally Define His Afterlife Beliefs

W hat's Next? I mean, the BIG MYSTERIOUS...WHAT'S NEXT? What will be next after I take my last breath? What will happen to me?

Some people believe nothing exists after we expire. Your body will be buried or burned, and the only continuation of your existence will be in government records, perhaps on a genealogy website, or with memories of loved ones or friends, maybe if you've published a book or become a well-known performer or had a building or city street named after you.

Other people believe that our consciousness or soul continues into some realm after we die. There are a lot of different thoughts about this in terms of what these realms are like.

It seems most major religions such as Christianity, Islam and Judaism — all have some form of divine judgment, where depending on how you've lived your life, you will gain some form of reward or punishment. Some of these religions talk about heaven or hell — and different theories within sects of these different religions and others describe all kinds of different levels of existence, planes of existence, but most define heaven or paradise for those who are deemed good, hell or hades or the underworld of shadows, punishment or torture for those who have been bad, committed terrible acts, or even had non-faithful thoughts.

The religions of Ancient Egypt required you to recite spells, formulae and passwords from the Book of the Dead in order to get into heaven. Damn, I can't even remember my passwords that allow me to open various software or online programs!

Some religions believe that all souls are cleansed, redeemed and become better after we die, no matter how terrible the acts that were committed. I do like the benevolence of these beliefs.

Some religions and philosophies believe in angels. Another religion believes Buddha mentors benevolent gods and goddesses. But think about this: There are these different sects for example, just in Christianity — and quite a few of the other religions. It seems like different religious leaders, mostly men, therefore mostly patriarchal, wanted to put their own stamp on the beliefs of what goes on or does not go on after we die. I think it is interesting, still, that most of these major religions have these common themes of divine judgment, reward and punishment, heaven or hell, the soul or consciousness continuing after we die, and various levels of existence. It's like all these regions derived from the same sources, just a little different depending on the tribes or nation-states one belonged to.

Does this mean religions, philosophies and what the afterlife might be, have more to do with politics, egotism, and patriarchy — at least in societies of the past 2000+ years, except for maybe a few places, like where Wonder Woman came from...or did that place begin more than 2000 years ago? Though the real question might be does it still exist hidden in some secret dimension, even in this earth realm? I hope so.

I am beginning to develop a different view of what the afterlife is, and I feel alright about expressing it. I'm not trying to convince anyone, or start a church. It's all up for discussion, right? A spiritual mystery nobody knows for sure. Until the last breath is taken. Or until one of these gods or goddesses, Wonder Woman, or just caring essences comes back to visit us from the afterlife to tell us what is real or unreal in after life dimensions. While we wait for that visit, let's put our souls together and see if we can reach a spiritual consensus. Or is that even important? Maybe there are as many afterlife dimensions as there are all the different religions, sects of religions, and anti-religions have imagined...if that's true perhaps after we pass from this earth realm, we can choose to exist in whatever dimension we have imagined the afterlife to be. Then, if that's true, I choose to imagine a positive holistically benevolent afterlife as positive. Even if none of what I imagine is true, then while I am alive at least I've lived a life in which I not only considered the well-being of others just as much as my own being, I have also lived life with a spiritual sense of joy that transcends the fear of death.

The Neophyte Seeker's Attempt to Finally Define His Afterlife Beliefs #2

(Beyond the patriarchal dark veils)

Many people are afraid of leaving this world to enter its unknown darkness. Some people just don't want to think about it. Some people are afraid there is nothing beyond this life. A nothingness — life ends, we end.

Some people feel there is a hierarchy of good and bad realities, and in between there are holding grounds for those people whose behavior is not acceptable but not bad enough to be sent for eternal punishment, or good enough to be allowed into the exquisitely pleasant dimensions. Even if an individual's behavior is not extreme one way or another, some gods or goddesses or higher beings have to hold most people accountable despite the notions of forgiveness in most of their religions. If you follow the rules in the reality of life before death, and become financially successful, according to some religions you most certainly will be allowed to transcend to the higher levels of the heavenly realms — even if you beat your spouse (this is not gender specific, though I am aware of statistics), harm others through greed, ignore abuse, etc. If you are successful, some people feel that's the key to the better religious life after this materially good life no matter what you've done.

If you are poor in this life before death, and break the law, and are alone and have been abused...if you are middle class that serves bosses and make shit wages, just as in past societies you are a serf that serves kings and queens, you may find yourself sentenced to what some people call purgatory in one of the patriarchal religions, just because they may need servants in their form of the afterlife...

THAT'S NOT ACCEPTABLE FROM MY SPIRITUAL PERSPECTIVE! LET'S FORM A PURGATORY PROTEST MOVEMENT!

I wonder how many individuals would choose to exist in the judgmental dimensions of various religions — especially if they would risk being sent to a concentration camp in purgatory or burning forever in a hellish place? Just wondering...

Then there is the thought that you keep coming back, are reborn into the physical reality where you have been forced to live many lives before — reincarnation — to continue to struggle to evolve until you reach a state of purity in which you so-call *evolve* back into the womb of the universe where your consciousness is *dissolved* and your unique identity is washed away, and you never have to exist with your unique spark of individual consciousness ever again — and never have to struggle in this sensual earth realm again...

TO QUOTE SOME STRANGE WIZARD I MET AT A FESTIVAL, "WHERE'S THE NONSENSICAL FUN IN THAT?"

I like my memories of my loves and my accomplishments — even my screw-ups. I don't want to lose who I am, especially when I become more evolved and want to contribute consciously to the well-being of others and all other essences of beings in all realms and dimensions. Give me a break...actually, I'll just break away from the idea that cycles end. I'll look forward to the spiral of evolution of consciousness in continuing cycles of being.

Let me enjoy an interactive collective with the infinite inter-elations of other evolving essences of being. Oh, does that sound too egotistical, not willing to allow my Self to dissolve? I certainly wouldn't just be thinking of my Self, but of all other essences of being in other dimensions I am going with to contribute to the continual well-being of...of all life and afterlife...though why wouldn't it be ok to enjoy my Self as I become a more evolved compassionate and caring being?

I've come to believe in the spiritual vision that multiple dimensions reflect different sides of ourselves. I like the concept that we remain who we have become and are becoming in this and other dimensions after and even during this life before death.

I like to imagine that we carry our unique consciousness with us after we die, and that as we transcend we become more aware, more cosmically balanced and evolved with the assistance of many other evolved beings — not just some omnipotent god-goddess-androgynous beings — even though I don't mind if such beings exist, if they are truly wise and benevolent in ways that help each being keep actualizing their spiritual potentials — which in my belief does not relate to a hierarchy, but reflects more complete and balanced levels of wholeness and wisdom.

I like to imagine that after we leave this earth realm, we become exquisitely aware and experience the blend of what we know and don't know.

We don't have to be afraid of what is behind what is referred to as the dark veil. We will be able to keep our own light shining as we blend with the lights of other essences — in loving and caring ways.

I'm still searching, but I am feeling more peaceful about the spiritual aspect of the afterlife.

Resurrecting or Reincarnating?

Will I resurrect as a zombie — that's not actually resurrecting in religious terms, is it? What is a zombie, though, in spiritual terms? Hollywood, graphic novels and other stories seem to depict zombies as bodies without souls or minds — well, what causes them to move around and focus on sounds or whatever? Some lower functioning parts of their brains? What happened to their psyche? Their souls?

Obviously, something is still working...so are they really dead?

To speculate, let's say I will reincarnate as a zombie and remain in the earth realm...or as a beetle or as my next evolved self with my consciousness the same...hmm, what can I do to make sure I don't become a zombie or beetle (not that I have anything against beetles) in the next incarnation?

The concept of resurrection is a part of a religious dogma that believes Jesus will return to earth to wake us up from our death sleep, and a perhaps save us from going to hell. From my perspective this concept is a myth or metaphor taken too literally — I don't believe in the concept of Hell. In a way, the various monolithic religious concepts of resurrection seem related to the eastern religious concepts of reincarnation, though totally dependent on Jesus finally returning from the dead.

Reincarnation involves a choice each essence of being will have after they transition into the afterlife. But after my death, if I had to choose between going to some hellish place or reincarnating as a beetle, I will obviously quickly choose to come back as a beetle. Sorry to mix metaphors...I mean religions...

We will transition into the afterlife with our evolving consciousness intact. Evolvement in the earth realm too often depicts becoming better than others. I rather like the concept of evolvement as meaning growing in understanding that does not make someone better than others, maybe just more informed, more willing to search for meaning beyond dogma that only enhances a few, or a few that belong to a certain religion or political belief system. In spiritual terms, some essences might choose to reincarnate during their process of evolving and develop new sides of self in positive ways.

When I Die — Collective Caring and Contributing

I will initially be sad to leave this earth realm at a time when more and more people are becoming evolved enough to rise above their conditioned, desperate selfish tribal ways in order to become more compassionate and inclusive of the exquisite array of diversity of all life forms and of the multitude of unique expressions.

I will initially be sad to leave this earth at a time when more and more people are making kind and caring connections with others, and are willing to share with all living essences to enhance the collective well-being.

For one brief transcendental moment, I will wish I could have stayed around to finally experience and contribute to this collective evolution of acceptance and caring and well-being...but I will know I can look forward to whatever opportunities to contribute to all that exists as I transition into beyond life dimensions and/or in my next physical realm life form, if I choose to incarnate.

Matthew's Attempted Suicide

M atthew was 23 when he decided he needed to leave this world. He felt overwhelmed by so many things in his life. He was alienated from his family. His attempts at relationships had totally been one failure after another. He never felt comfortable going to counseling during the years his parents forced him to. Now that he had been living alone since he left his parent's home a few years ago, he had never felt so...alone.

He had friends...sort of friends...but he felt nobody understood him. He felt he was alien on this earth, and wished he lived on another planet, in another dimension...and that's when he decided to just kill himself...and hope that wherever that would lead would be better than where he was.

So he planned it. He didn't like the idea of using a gun to shoot himself in his mouth or brain...how gross, he thought.

He thought about jumping off of a bridge, but knew he couldn't go through with it because he was intensely afraid of heights. He had always thought mountain climbing was crazy, beyond his comprehension.

And he thought, "Oh god, I could never hang myself or drown myself. I'm such a squeamish coward. How am I going to kill myself if I can't stand the pain of it?"

Then, Matthew decided on taking a bunch of pills. He had dismissed this earlier because he only was taking anti-depressants, and was worried that if it didn't work, he would be cut off — but then he eventually decided he needed to take a risk to free himself from his emotional pain...

So one night, when the moon was full, which didn't really mean anything to him spiritually or esoterically, (because he didn't know what that meant) — but he liked the light it shone on his apartment balcony and gave him the light in his darkened bedroom to find the other pills he had stolen from his parents and various friends. He didn't even know what these pills were, but he felt since he had a bunch of them, he would certainly be able to die and leave this fucking earth, goddammit!

After he watched a rerun of the *The Office,* which he had watched many, many times — perhaps too many times in his young life, he began taking his pills. He then lay on his bed, and begin to feel sleepy...sleepy...sleepy...

And he experienced transitioning through darkness, and then into a brilliant light! He later remembered he wished he had his sunglasses...

Then he came face to face with this bearded man whom he felt he would never have ever hung out with, but somehow seemed comforting to him...

He said, "Matthew, you have made a foolish decision...to try to kill yourself just because you feel overwhelmed."

"But I do feel overwhelmed. I can't handle life..."

"Ok, but let's sort this through...I see in your future that you will meet a woman with whom you will fall deeply in love and whom you will marry and have three wonderful children. You will open a restaurant, and will be successful and will live a long happy life — well, that's one of your timelines..."

"What kind of a restaurant?" Matthew asked.

"What does matter?"

"I'm very particular what I eat."

"You'll get over it...and anyway you will have a choice."

Matthew felt confused, and said "Ok, maybe I shouldn't have tried to kill myself. But what can I do about it now that I've already done it?"

"You haven't already done it. Haven't you heard of near-death experiences?"

"Of course."

"So I'll send you back...and you will wake up in a hospital with your stomach pumped. It won't be a pleasant experience. But remember this pleasant encounter if you ever feel like killing yourself again. Death is not something you should strive for, but also should not fear. Oh, and when you come back alive...say nice things about me...the crazy old spirit you met, but actually, I prefer to be just called Wily Wizard.

Anna's Assisted Suicide

A nna walked out of her doctor's office after he told her she had lung cancer and probably would only have less than a year to live. He described the symptoms she would possibly be experiencing and the types of medications she would need to help her to cope with the pain. He tried to assure her that she would be able to remain comfortable during the last days.

As soon as she left his office, Anna decided she was not going to end her life with the kind of death in which she would just be kept alive...though in a state of being that would not allow her to function with all her capacities. She thought that kind of death would not be so *kind*...

During her previous job as a caregiver, she had been present at the death of a number of people who died of lung cancer, and some were content that they had lived as long as they could. She knew she was not like that. She had decided long ago if she had a terminal illness, she would choose assisted suicide as a way of choosing when and how she would die.

She was no longer a caregiver. She became a dog walker a few years earlier to supplement her social security retirement income. She loved dog walking...connecting with the varied personalities of the dogs and the physical exercise, being outdoors, and having some flexibility of hours of work.

She knew, though, that she would not be able to continue walking dogs for others as her cancer progressed. She decided to prepare for choosing her time to die before she became so incapacitated with pain and drugs that she would not be able to experience life in the way she wanted to — sharing with her friends, gardening, being physically active, enjoying going to concerts. She knew she would be able to do many of these things, even as she progressed through her illness, but she had decided she wanted to leave her life on earth on her own terms.

Anna had lived alone for many years. She devoted her life to interacting with her friends, mostly women friends, though she did have very close men friends. She also had devoted her life to her own dogs, though it had been a while since she had her own animals. Her dog walking had provided her the connections to these precious animals that she treasured. For many years, she enjoyed living alone in her house and being independent.

Anna's first task was to find a doctor who would support her choice for assisted suicide. In Oregon, she did have a doctor whom she thought would be willing to support her choice. She talked with him and he said he would support her decision.

Then she decided she wanted to gather a group of her women friends who would be present at her passing. She envisioned a ceremony with her women friends surrounding her as she lay in her bed and before she drank the medication that would allow her to drift away. She was not religious, but she believed she would be flowing into a lovely spiritual place, and looked forward to experiencing the joys of a body free of pain, and a soul free to embrace the wonderment of what comes next.

She contacted eight of her close women friends, and all agreed to be present with her. She had meetings with them over the months following her diagnosis to prepare and plan the ceremony of her passing.

She had already given her precious belongings to her various friends — her CDs, some of her artwork, jewelry and books. She had been enjoying her life fully until this chosen date of her ceremony of passing. Anna had put it off as long as she could, but the feeling of pain began to increase. She was also happy with her decision to have the choice to determine when she would be passing with her close friends near her, sending her on her way.

A few months prior, she had begun to breathe more heavily and with more difficulty, experiencing more pain, which made her decide to define a date to die more peacefully.

When the day came that Anna had chosen to transcend from her life on earth, she woke up before sunrise. The ceremony was not scheduled to occur until sunset, but she wanted to experience the last day of her life in as full of way that she could. When she got up from her bed in the dark, she went into the front room, and started playing the album, *An Ancient Muse* by Loreena McKennitt. Anna lit the candle she had placed on a small table in the center on her living room and sat on the floor listening to the music and meditating on the candle light. At one point, she took the intricately-designed brass candle extinguisher, with a peacock on the top of the bell, that she had also placed on the table, and ended the light of the candle. She smiled to herself as she had long ago resisted using the phrase "candle snuffer to snuff out light." She continued smiling as she watched the thin trail of smoke ascend into the air. Then she relit the candle, and after a few moments of meditating on the flickering flame, she put out the light again and sat smiling in the darkness of the room. She continued this ritual a few more times.

Then before dawn, she started playing, *Here Comes the Sun/Inner Light,* from the Beatles' Love album. She didn't want to leave her life in this world, but she felt mixtures of exhilaration and peacefulness as she took a long bubble bath with candles and incense and the harmonious gypsy choral songs from *Bulgarian Voices* playing in the background. As she got dressed, she kept in mind visions of transcending into an afterlife that she had become to recognize as liberating as well as embracing and comforting.

She made her favorite green tea, and then ate a light breakfast of yogurt and blue berries with toast and honey. She washed her dishes, and cleaned the counter. Then turned around, and looked at the interior of her house. She planned on spending the day reflecting on all the decorations she had designed and created in her living space, as well as the photographs that captured special moments of her life — these decorations, artwork and photographs all attached to memories of creativity, of sharing, of loving, and of an exuberance of living and being.

She cried often as the day progressed, not with feelings of despair but with feelings of profound appreciation for what life has provided for her, and what she has been able to develop within herself, a maturity that allowed her to experience fully opportunities and learn from challenges. As she experienced her last day in this realm — walking around her house and remembering the special moments of her past — she continued to feel satisfied with her life on earth, and felt ready to move on.

Before her friends arrived to participate in the ceremony, she first walked outside on her back porch to look, one final time, at the garden she had planted and cared for through so many years. She began weeding and lightly pruning some of the bushes. Even though she was having difficulty breathing, she stayed in her garden for over an hour, sometimes just sitting on the ground. With caring feelings, she looked at each of the array of the flowers, bushes, and the herbs in her garden for long periods of time, and said goodbye to each — including the spikes of the blue star-shaped Camassia, the pink, red and white flowers of the Lewisa, the velvety shades of lilac and rose of the Satin Flowers, and her Rosemary and Sage herbs.

Anna finally stood and looked up at the blue sky. She had decided she wanted to die just as the light of the day was entering into the darkness of the night. She was not afraid of the darkness. As she looked up into clear blue sky, she smiled and gave a blessing to the lightness that she knew she would be transiting into. She felt the loveliness and expanse of the blue sky freeing her soul, and felt herself breathing more peacefully, and with less pain, than she had recently been experiencing. She coughed and felt the taste of blood which had become a familiar experience. Anna stood up, and then waved goodbye to the blue sky as she went inside again to wait for her friends to eventually arrive.

When she went inside, she put on another playlist of her favorite songs, including the Beatles, *All Across the Universe* and *On Our Way Home (Two of Us)*, and other songs by Joni Mitchell, Fleetwood Mac, Willie Nelson, Aimee Mann, Be Good Tanyas, Neal Young, Crosby, Stills & Nash and others. She continued walking around her house, singing softly. She felt she was acknowledging and saying final goodbyes to the spirit beings within all of the paintings, clothes, crafts, and photographs representing her life. She felt fulfilled and appreciative of all that she had experienced and that all she endured and overcame, all she had loved, all she had created, all she had shared with others, and all of life.

As her friends arrived, each brought a flower, and each flower was put into a vase of Anna's. They didn't go right away into her bedroom for the ceremony and transition. Until each of her friends arrived, they sat in her front room listening to the music she was playing, and talked about her life. She shared memories of how she had met each of her friends, and what she appreciated about each of them. They in turn shared their own special memories of their interactions over the years. There were tears, but also smiles and laughter...they had all prepared for this, and all felt Anna's passing was a spiritual experience.

After all of her friends had arrived, and before sunset, Anna stood up and invited everyone to come with her into her bedroom. Anna had put chairs around her bed, and invited her friends to sit where they wanted to. She then went into the bathroom and changed into a loose, white flowing gown. The scent of sandalwood incense floated through the room. Anna came back into her bedroom, pulled back the covers and slid into her bed. She looked up at the ceiling art she had painted long ago of the Sun and the Moon and smiled. As had been arranged when she was ready, she started chanting, and her friends in the room joined in. Each came up to her one by one and nestled their cheeks against her.

Before the moment of sunset, she reached over and took a container of liquid medication. All of Anna's friends touched her body and her soul as she drank the fluid...and then she slowly closed her eyes and passed away into the light of release and spiritual joy, where she was embraced and experienced a sensation of peaceful being without physical pain.

Would You Ever Choose Physician Assisted Suicide?

The increase in the life spans of humans can mean people have continued opportunities to share with their loved-ones, enjoy their own accomplishments, and explore new potentials of being. But it can also mean living longer with disease, pain and dementia.

Living longer is possibly allowing individuals to have more years of enjoying the fullness of life in the earth realm — with all the loving interactions with others, sensual pleasures, joys of culture and nature, and spiritual attunement. But what happens when one's quality of life is compromised by the body falling apart, and the individual experiencing more moments of pain than moments of joyful existence and activities?

Individuals will have to decide what physical struggles they want or are able to endure that will still allow them to live a "quality of life" as they live longer.

There are political and moral issues related to this question. The inequality of income, as well as racial and religious bigotry, has caused higher death rates for certain populations and those living in poverty or with limited access to quality health care. Also, some scientists believe that one day it will be possible for life spans to increase to 150+ years. Will our earth be able to handle this increase? These are issues that need to be addressed.

I want to live life to the fullest for as long as I can. Suicide has never been something I have contemplated, though I have supported the "right to die" if a person so chooses. I believe it is a spiritual choice that we have, to not just honor in general, but also to personally contemplate if and when we might make our own choice to decide when to transcend into the afterlife.

If I Could Choose How I Would Die

I would hope to die before I've lost the capacity to experience a quality of life, activities in life that give you joy — singing, dancing, enjoying other people, being able to read, being able to recognize my love ones, and being creative or useful or engaged...

I would hope to die without experiencing sustained physical suffering or pain or at least having developed the spiritual awareness that I will be transcending my pain as I transition into the afterlife...

I would hope to be ready when I can see the other side — it would be spiritually transforming to be conscious of seeing the other side when I'm needing to go...

Though I know I have no control about the when and circumstances of passing I will have (right now my goal is I don't plan on choosing assisted suicide but I've come to believe that there may be circumstances that might make this a right choice). But despite what suffering I may endure as I die, I hope I have enough cognitive awareness to be able to reflect on:

What I feel good about in my life, and what I have accomplished, what joys have I experienced, and what sides of myself I have developed as a result of my disappointments, mistakes...

What I learned and how resilient I was able to be as I worked to overcome my life challenges and take advantage of opportunities and memories of engaged interactions with my love ones and ways, I was able to contribute in some ways, even little ways, and...

The well-being of others in our world.
And to open my consciousness to the afterlife dimensions I will be journeying into.

As the Ten-Year-Old Girl Dies

As she was drifting away from an illness she was born with, she remembered why she chose her mother...she knew she was being born into a body that would not be in normal health, and that she would experience challenges other children would not have to face, and that she would probably die young. She had chosen to come into this world, this body for her own spiritual reasons, not because she had to.

One reason she chose to be born the way she had was because of the opportunity to spend some time with the mother she had also chosen. She had recognized that the mother she had chosen was someone who could give her the gift of emotional and spiritual resilience...someone who would nurture and care for her, attend to her needs, but also someone who would encourage her to be all she could be, to rise above the limitations of her body...to develop herself as fully as she could while she lived.

This gift of spiritual resilience was something the ten-year-old girl wanted to experience in her own journey to develop the fullness of her being.

The ten-year-old girl had lived other lifetimes, and had experienced many lives in physical bodies. She had lived and died at different ages, once living into the 9th decade. She had been able to continue to develop different sides of her spiritual consciousness, not just through her lives in different physical bodies, but also through her interactive blending with other essences of being in the many dimensions she had journeyed through.

But when she became aware of the woman whom she chose to be her mother, she felt compelled to be born through her, and to experience growing and developing in her presence, with her guidance, with her exuberance for living, and with her spiritual resilience.

Was she being selfish to want to spend time with someone who she would be giving some difficult child-rearing challenges? She knew she was not being selfish, just enjoying the opportunities that all essences of being can choose to experience as they continue to develop different sides of their consciousness in the afterlife.

As the essence of being who had lived for ten years as a girl with a physical disability drifted away, she felt so happy to have experienced life with her upbeat mom...her mom who had helped her transcend her disability. She knew that the loving bonds she had formed with her mother in now her past life would continue to exist throughout lifetimes and existences in beyond life dimensions...and that they would flow together often, both while her mother was still living, and after she passes...with the joys of spiritual resilience.

What Would I Regret When I Die?

One of the definitions of regret is… "To be very sorry for." This is related to guilt…

I realize actions that create harm, violent physical or emotional harm or abuse can evoke a valid regret. But what of most other choices that others may be sad about?

Or

What of other behavior that does not mean to cause harm?

What about other behavior that reflects a psychological illness?

What about just missing an opportunity?

What about not being aware enough to change one's behavior, which then causes the loss of a love relationship or a career?

In these instances, did we learn anything? If we didn't, then we will as we transcend into the afterlife…

The afterlife has nothing to do with punishment, with increasing one's regrets, or one's guilt. Existing in such beyond life dimensions while we are living and after we pass allows each of us to find the loving core of our soul which we all carry within us. It dissolves regrets, guilty feelings and even transgressions and abuses into pools of not only forgiveness, but also spiritual healing…no action in the earth realms is a result of some ominous ingrained evilness in the human spirit. It's the result of the physical, emotional, educational, sexual, economical, racial and other abuses of others in the earth realm, and these abuses are transcended and healed in the beyond life dimensions.

If You Feel You've Been Left Behind

We are all aware of the process of grieving, even if we haven't yet prepared before for the passing of our love ones. There is, of course, a deep feeling of loss when a child, a parent, an intimate love partner, or a close friend passes into other realms.

There is that common grieving process...but what if we've learned to practice the process before a person dies? What if we have learned to connect with beyond life dimensions before experiencing death of loved ones or ourselves? What if we've learned to stay connected with our loved ones while they are living in this earth realm reality when they are not in our physical presence?

If you feel you've been left behind, then you might have been living too much through the other person, and may be choosing to develop your own positive sense of being...

If you feel you've been left behind, look up to the stars at night and see beyond the stars and look into your dreams at night...you will be able to envision and feel visitations and connections surrounding and comforting your psyche, transforming your feelings of grief.

If You Feel You've Been Left Behind by the Death of Your Love Partner

Hold on to your feelings of love —

Remember when you first looked into the eyes of your love partner who has passed.

Remember times you made love together when you were able to blend together sensually and emotionally...and then after you both culminated your intimacy you both turned together on your sides, again looking into each other's eyes, lingering with the joy of your souls and bodies blended in ways that transcended time, transcended the death of separation in this lifetime to allow a being of intimacy beyond the limits of the body.

You have not been left behind by your love partner. You will be able experience new memories based on the memories of experiences you've made together.

Develop your spiritual awareness of how you are and will continue to be surrounded by your love partner who will always be with you...

Ghosts

D
o the essences of beings — ghosts — hang around the earth realm after an individual dies?

Some people believe so. Maybe it is so...how do we know? Some people feel they are being haunted, but could these feelings of being haunted just be a symptom of a profound sense of loss, of an individual not wanting to let go of a loved one who has passed, or a symptom of paranoia or psychosis?

While I have a positive and optimistic view of the afterlife, I accept that some essences of being may choose, may have reasons to hang around after death for good or not so good reasons...

If that is so, I also believe that individuals who are living in the earth realm can set spiritual boundaries between troubled essences of being who passed — ghosts — who need to be freed to transition into the healing afterlife. I know there are liberating techniques that people who are spiritually attuned can use to help free the souls caught in this realm.

Let's free these spirits if they are caught. Let's help them become fully liberated... Let's give them their freedom to enter beyond life dimensions where they will be healed and enhanced in a spiritual loving way by all who have ever existed.

Let's give them a cosmic hug and send them on their more spiritually liberated ways...

Transforming Grief

Transforming grief involves being able to continue to feel connected with the souls, the spirits, and the sweet and loving memories of loved ones you have lost...to be able to continue to feel connected when living with their physical presences is no longer possible...

We all know transforming grief takes time, and takes a variety of inner and interactive resources to make such a healing emotional and spiritual transformation. The feeling of emotional pain as you remember the loss of the physical presence of your loved one who has passed can be triggered at any time...but like any emotional pain we may feel, we all have the capacity to transform the pain into sweet joys of memories, and then into a reaffirming appreciation of the enduring connection with your loved one that never will be lost...

The Death Tarot Card

Lately I keep drawing the Death card when I lay out my early morning meditation using tarot cards to assist me in capturing the meaning of the moment and of the coming day.

The Death card...what does this archetypal metaphysical card mean? I don't believe you can think of the Death card without thinking of what comes next — a rebirth...I can imagine that for a person not used to contemplating this archetype, the Death card might be unsettling...transformative change can be unsettling.

But through our lives we need at times to let things go in order to begin again, or to free ourselves from patterns of behavior, relationships, careers, and locations that no longer reflect our beings and potentials. In this way letting something die is the first step in a transformation, a transition that leads to something more meaningful...and learning to let things die with appreciation and peace can lead to our transitions into the afterlife with accepting and peaceful anticipations. Death is not something to fear — we can transform this fear with spiritual understanding and with the embrace of a transcendental awareness...

A Man Transcends as a Result of a Heart Attack

Walter, a 63-year-old man, felt he had lived a good life, mostly healthy with no major bouts of illnesses or injuries that were life threatening or lasting very long. Yet a few years ago, he began feeling more and more physical symptoms and he became quite concerned.

At night he would feel discomfort in his chest if he lay on his left side, and if he turned onto his back or right side, the chest pain would go away. Four or five times a week, Walter walked a half-hour or more around his neighborhood, and sometimes he would briefly feel a mild chest pain and shortness of breath for a brief period of time. For many years he had well-controlled high blood pressure and high cholesterol with medication, diet and exercise. Both his mother and father had died of heart problems. Walter had talked with his primary care physician about some of the symptoms he was feeling, but blood, stress, EKG and various vascular scanning tests were relatively normal.

When Walter started having his symptoms and concerns, as he lay on his in his bed on many nights ready to fall asleep, he would become fearful of having a heart attack. He imagined suddenly experiencing an intense pain in his chest that would exist for a terribly frightening few moments before death would finally pull him into the afterlife...and hopefully into some relief from the pain. But it was those few desperate and painful minutes before passing that he became fearful of experiencing death. He didn't want to leave as long as he could function with the energy and vitality he was used to feeling.

He lived alone, and he wondered what those seconds or minutes before death would be like...would he have time to call 911? Would he have time to think about the life he was leaving? He had a smart watch that was supposed to enable him to alert someone if he was having a medical emergency, but he had never gotten around to programming it.

As a result of these fears, about a year and a half ago, Walter decided to seek ways to relieve his fears. He sought guidance from a meditation and yoga teacher who taught him deep breathing, relaxation and visualization techniques. These techniques relieved his fears, especially because he became able, at times, to envision that he was connecting with and visiting beyond life dimensions and the afterlife. When he lay in bed at night and began to feel fearful of having a heart attack, he would focus on his peaceful connections with spiritual dimensions, and his fears quickly dissolved.

During his meditative visits into beyond life dimensions, he had connected with his wife and others of his family and friends who had previously passed away and this gave him spiritual comfort and joy.

On the morning he passed from a heart attack, Walter had woken up from a restful night's sleep. He had stayed in bed a little longer than usual, and could see the morning light flowing into his room through the edges of the window shades. He felt excited about embracing the day.

Walter got up from his bed, and as he started to walk to the front room, he felt an intense pain in his chest, felt disoriented, and as he clutched his chest, fell back onto the bed.

He took a deep breath and thought about trying to call someone, but then he decided if this was his time to transcend, he could accept it. He didn't fear the unknown of afterlife, because he had visited beyond life dimensions quite often, and knew how peaceful and spiritually uplifting he had felt each time he did. He looked forward to continuing to see and connect with loved ones who had previously passed.

These thoughts occurred during the seconds before Walter passed and right before he passed, he envisioned images of loved ones and others who had passed waiting and welcoming him. He felt the touch of the familiar hands of his wife cuddling his cheeks. Walter's last feeling and thought before losing consciousness and transcending was of a serene sense of appreciation that he had learned to connect with the afterlife while living.

I'm Not Afraid of the Darkness of Death

I'm not afraid of what may seem like the forever darkening of the light of the Sun in this wonderful realm of existence. Because I have seen the light that remains beyond the sunset, beyond the cycles of day and night, waking and sleeping, dying and transcending...an expansive light that emanates warmly from spiritual dimensions beyond the darkness surrounding my soul — just across the veiled shadows — as we travel into and through the shadows, just as each night we can enter into the vivid dream worlds and then wake up refreshed each dawn, we will always come again into the light...as we realize the light has always remained within our souls even during the darkness, which is a regenerating contrast of the ever brightness within our essences of being.

In my life I have been used to flowing with the dance of the night and day, light and darkness throughout the seasons, and know that where there is darkness there is also always light — when darkness comes light will follow with a warm and cozy embrace, I have experienced the spiritual interplay between darkness and light, death and rebirth.

Darkness is not something to fear, it is something to be soothed by...it is the passageway to the rebirth of one's being, of one's essence into beyond life dimensions of another realm.

I'm not afraid to die, just as I've never been afraid to go to sleep in the darkness of the night.

I'm Not Afraid of the Darkness of Death #2

I 'm not scared by the darkness of death. I have become aware that the darkness is just a passageway that will open up into expanses of lovely, warm and embracing colors... darkness is a passageway where dreams are envisioned, where healing occurs, where rebirth into new phases begin. Darkness is not something to fear.

Darkness represents a time to lay your soul down on a pillow of dreams and to rest before your essence begins again in a rebirth of ever-expanding ways of being...

I'm not afraid to die. While I don't seek to transition from this dynamic and wonderful earth realm, I have been developing myself through spiritual contemplation and reflection to welcome what comes next with an open soul — my soul, my unique consciousness open to blending more fully with the embrace and compassionate love of all who have transitioned before — and with a hope, especially, of connecting with you, my love, and with other family and friends who have passed before.

I'm Not Afraid of the Darkness of Death #3

I'm not scared by the darkness — of what might be unknown in the shadows. I've always imagined sparkling crystals and flowering spirits inhabiting the darkness where another beautiful reality exists.

I'm not scared by the darkness because I refuse to be a victim — I'm never going to be a victim. I will always rise above the actions of the abusive, the bigoted, the uninformed...even if I'm killed by hatred or by accident, I know the darkness is where transcendence lies.

To float above my death,
    To rise above my pain,
        To rise above the harm that someone
            may have caused me.

I will always exist with the cosmic courage and comfort that I have been given by the light and love that exists, and enhances, darkness in the spiritual dimensions.

I'm not afraid of the darkness as I envision the continued healing embrace of all the loving essences who will be waiting for me in the afterlife.

Before I Die — I Want to Take Spiritual Risks

I want to take opportunities within the moments I have left to be creatively active, and to be contributing what I can to the well-being of my family, my friends and others who have contributed to my own well-being...

All my life, I have attempted to balance risk-taking with security. We all need to have some foundation of security, but we have to be willing to take risks drawing on our comfort zones, our security foundations, to allow us to take the risks we need to take to become all we are meant to be, to develop our potentials in this life before we transcend...

Maybe the biggest risk is exploring and accepting death, and then using the awareness and acceptance gained to allow us to enjoy each moment we are living in this realm.

The biggest risk might be allowing ourselves to be open to the darkness, the closing of our eyes knowing we may not open them again in our present life form...the risk to take a chance, to open to the spiritual possibilities of entering into the light of afterlife dimensions that could bathe us in a nurturing and joy beyond what we have experienced before...the risk of opening ourselves to the unknown dimensions, which can become known. We have guides...spiritual guides living among us, and other spiritual guides that visit us in our night and day dreams...in all those moments when we lose sight of only our own ego, and think of the desires and needs of others...

Before I die and while I am living, I want to take the risks of opening myself to the unknown, and accepting as I enter the initial darkness of not knowing where I will be going. There will be a light that will be comforting me, nurturing me and showing me the way to the exuberant risks I have to take to allow my essence to unfold and become all I am meant to be in the infinite dimensions of existence.

Wonders of Living and Dying

I lie next to you as you near the end of your life, and treasure the moments I can look into your eyes, hug you and listen to music as we both fall asleep.

I found a photograph of us visiting friends in our first trip overseas...it wasn't to Europe, which is where all of our travels since have been to...but it was to Katmandu, Nepal.

We were walking by a river. I remembered seeing the bodies of people who had died and were being burned to release their souls. The spirituality, reverence and beauty of the moment has stayed with me over the years, and now in my older age, and finally seeing through my ego blinders of wanting to go on and on, I have recognized that living life to the fullest embraces leaving this life to become more than we could ever be living in this earth. I still think living in this earth realm can be pretty sweet, especially as I lie with you, looking deeply into your eyes and into your soul.

I'm not trying to take anything away from living fully in this life. Why would I, unless I am not living life fully? I recognize that spiritual wonders are not just limited to this life...there is so much more...and the wonders in the afterlife may be what makes anything we've hoped for become fulfilled with transcendental joy.

Who Will Be Waiting for Me After I Die?

Y ou, my love, I hope, but I don't want you to just be hanging around if you have a special journey you should be going on, exploring, enjoying in your new existence to become more, to be more. Don't wait for me, I will look for you and hopefully will find you if that's meant to be.

I wonder if our exquisite sharing in our lives together on earth before we died...I wonder if that was our time to give each other the gifts of growth and development that we were meant to give each other, and that now we need to move on after we transcend to experience other beings with whom we can further share gifts of spiritual growth?

Yet I still hope to see you at some point in this other dimensional journey. After all, I've always considered you my cosmic companion...

I hope you will be waiting for me, my love, but will I recognize you? Surely, I will recognize your spirit, or the essence of who you are. The essence of your inner smile — the essence of your spiritual embrace that perhaps I will only be able to feel with my inner sensuality that may transcend touch...

I know you will be waiting for me, my love, because you never really left me. I have always felt you around me...but I want to join you in the essence of being that you are, and explore what my freed soul essence can allow us to share in our spiritually liberated forms. That excites me and transcends my sadness for having to be separated from our present for a while...

Dream That You Were Waiting for Me After I Died

I dreamed that after I died you were waiting for me, just as I had hoped...you, the love of my life on earth, were waiting for me. I could feel your presence before I could see you — and seeing is not the right expression, perhaps sensing you...and then I dreamed you surrounded me with your love and comfort — familiar from memories of us lying in each other's arms, our souls surrounding each other. In my dream, after I died, and you were waiting for me, I experienced a union that transcended the intertwining of our bodies and souls during our emotional and physical lovemaking in the earth realms before each of us passed.

In my dream, when I died and you came into my presence you created visions of sweet-scented flowers and sounds of the most exquisite music — both visions and sounds filled me with happiness and contentment.

In my dream you let me know that we would be flowing here and there together, but we would also be flowing in different directions often as we continued on our own separate journeys. You let me know that in the other dimensions in which we are traveling, there is no either/or, but each essence of being exists in union as well as separately from others, in conscious union with the collective spirits of existence of other life forms, and also with the conscious awareness of the uniqueness of each of our separate life forms.

In this dream, after I died you taught me that the union of love, in the realms beyond the limits of our life before death, is enhanced by all souls joining together as they flow in and out of these individual unions and as we each continue to experience the continued expressions and journeys from our individual perspectives.

What Do You Want to Leave Behind?

Your expressions of love for significant others, family and friends? How will you share these caring and loving feelings for those whom you have loved and have loved you over the years of your life?

Your creative expressions — art, writings, crafts, videos, photographs, recordings? Who will appreciate, keep, and share these expressions in ways that reflect your creative essence?

Your special possessions and memorabilia — photographs, gifts and letters from loved ones, jewelry, household items and art collected from travels, made by you and/or have given you pleasure over the years? Who will treasure these special possessions as much as you have in your life?

Your letters, journals, other personal writings? Who do you trust with such personal expressions of yourself?

Your mundane possessions — outdated financial records, clothes, shoes, drawers full of meaningless items, toothbrushes, old magazines, old outdated electronic equipment, etc., etc.? Are you expecting family and/or friends to dispose of these things for you?

Your assets? If you have minimal or no assets, then your decisions will be easy. If you have significant assets, then who will you leave them to?

Your body or your ashes? Do you want your body buried in a coffin, in the natural earth without a coffin, or do you want to be cremated? If cremated, what do you want to be done with your ashes — released in nature, released in some faraway place that was meaningful to you, buried somewhere that can be visited by family and friends, shared with lockets with those who might want to carry a memory of you with them?

Your reputation and legacy? You might need to develop a spiritual detachment about these concerns, accepting that you've done the best you could in this lifetime and will continue to evolve within beyond life dimensions.

As I Accept My Death, I Realize I Have Not Been Perfect

Why couldn't I be perfect at everything I tried...ok, ok. I know. I know...don't remind me... nothing is and no life form in the earth realm can be perfect. The flaws allow us to become better and to become fuller, to not succumb to an illusion of godlike narcissism (except for a narcissist who thinks he/she is a god and is perfect). The flaws allow us to realize that we all need each other to help to fill in the gaps of imperfection, to challenge and support each other, and to become more whole than we would be if we were just selfish asses (I debated using that word; asses may not always be perfect, but are necessary for our existence, but even debating this in my mind might be a bit anal).

Even if we are good at heart, congenial, sympathetic, or empathetic, there are times we are not so good, there are things we are not so good at...

As I die, I would like to accept my imperfections...and not dwell on them to the extent that I lose awareness of what I've accomplished in this life, of the times I've been helpful to others in a selfless way, of the love I have given to others, the smile and look in the eyes of others who I have felt connected with and hoped that they know I loved and appreciated their essences.

While I wait to see the light of the spiritual afterlife...not just for things I may not have done in a better way, I want to just be accepted for who I tried to be, and who I am, with the hope that I can continue to be better, healed and guided by those who can spiritually empower me to be my own inner guide one day...

What Do I Want People to Say About Me After I Die?

The question I feel more comfortable answering is, "What would I like to say about myself after I die?"

I was a loving family member, and treasured the opportunities involved in being a love partner, parent, grand-parent and great-grandparent — also a loving son, brother and extended family member. I cared for others and though a bit introverted, I enjoyed my interactions with my friends and close neighbors. I cared about the well-being of casual acquaintances and strangers, not just in my local community, but throughout the world.

I cherished romance and intimacy as important experiences and expressions in my life. While I was young, I realized I had a lot to learn about love, women's needs, and I worked at learning and becoming a more responsive love partner...which eventually allowed me to enter into the relationship with the woman who became my life partner...and we continued to not take anything for granted, especially each other's needs as we helped each other grow and continued to keep the fires of our romance intimacy strong throughout our lives together.

I was a person who sustained a sense of optimism about the evolving actualization of human potential — potentials related to people around the world caring about diversity of all races, ethnic, cultural, political, and religious ways of being...and hoped that political and religious viewpoints were also evolving toward more inclusiveness to avoid rejecting, subjugating or harming others who have different viewpoints.

I was a person whose sense of optimism and romance kept my fires of vigor and creativity burning brightly and warmly regardless of the struggles of circumstances and even the weather...

Ultimately, I tried to live a balanced life based upon the holistically comprehensive and inclusive model that I was fortunate to be exposed to as a young man. While I attempted to live a balanced life, I knew that a state of balance was a guiding principle and not something that could be achieved. I tried to learn from my mistakes, screw-ups, insensitivities, and blind spots, but did not let them extinguish my fires of love, intent, creativity and renewal when I woke to the joys, opportunities and challenges of each new day.

I loved all sorts of art — literary, visual, movies, streaming series, and music. I enjoyed science fiction, romance, and cathartic dramas. I particularly liked Star Trek episodes because of their positivity about humanity as well as their excellent story lines.

Later in life I realized that my concepts of spirituality related to connecting with beyond life dimension, not just with my abstract mind, but also with the fullness of my psyche and soul. I realized that dimensions of the afterlife needed to be brought more consciously into my day-to-day practice of being, and I was thankful for developing this consciousness and spiritual connection as I entered into the afterlife.

Spiritual Imagination

Don't be an extreme or imbalanced skeptic. Allow yourself to take rational risks and embrace dimensions beyond what you can see and measure. Develop your spiritual imagination of what you would like the afterlife to be.

1. Imagine the type of ethereal environment you'd like to be in. Notice the ambience of the surroundings that you envision, and what would allow you to feel peaceful.

2. If you could choose to be any personality or animal or being or inanimate object to blend with or inhabit for a while, what would you choose?

3. Imagine traveling to somewhere soothing, peaceful, comforting or dynamic, creative, romantic, exciting, or meaningful — or a blend of these feelings — the place you choose doesn't just have to be on earth.

4. Imagine you can make exploratory and evolving choices as you exist in a variety of spiritual dimensions in the afterlife.

Develop your spiritual imagination and attunement to the afterlife as a way of preparing for a positive passing, but don't use it to give fuel to your fears...use it to relax into the eventual possibilities of your death transition, into the afterlife where you will be able to create the choices of new aspects of your essence and fondly remember the joys of who you've been and what you've already experienced during your past existences.

Remember your joys in life — despite whatever struggles, pain and trauma you've endured, remember and visualize the times you've laughed with enjoyment; walked in nature and become one with the essence of natural beauty; danced, sang, listened and felt the liveliness of upbeat music or the peace and serenity of instrumentals and harmonies of the songs...

Spiritual Imagination and visualizations are precious gateways to connecting with the beyond life dimensions and preparing for a positive transition into the afterlife.

Spiritual Visualizations — Connecting With Spiritual Beyond Life Dimensions by Journaling

O n days Jonathan is not working at his job as a nurse at the hospital, he follows a special ritual that helps him to connect with creative spiritual realms. After getting dressed and eating breakfast with his love partner, he sits at the table and opens his journal. He reads what he has written on the inside cover:

Spirits of Words, I am open to receiving your guidance from beyond life dimensions...take my words where they want to go today...assist me in expressing what flows from spiritual dimensions to enhance what exists in all its various ways in my life in this earth realm.

On this day, after his partner left to do errands, he begins to write a stream of words without conscious thinking:

Orange blossoms opening through scents and unfolding petals of beauty I want to see spiritual gateways wherever I look deeply, transcend into the flowers of my garden, into your eyes when we are making love, into passages of a poetic book I am reading, experiencing cathartic transformations of actors in dramas about dying and death, about love and passion, about loss and gain — gaining, rearranging, readjusting to the changing strange tides as I make liquid strides, leaping flying weeping over barriers that have sometimes encased my consciousness, coming to me as dream images reflecting shadows that have been hiding deep within my unconscious until waking, never forsaking, never feigning what I should be raking as I clear away the debris of left over doubts and fears I have tried to shatter and then transform — though during these past moments I keep thinking about orange blossoms and now I feel myself wishing for citrus jam spread over warmed bread — then I look out my window and see you coming back from shopping I'm sure with a pastry that I know will be a warm apricot Danish croissant and I feel I have transcended in this life imagining it will be the same when I really transcend hoping for the existence of the best of transcendental pastries — who says we can't experience the imaginative joys of beyond life while we are living in this sensual earth realm?

Spiritual Connections Through Meditating in Nature

Every weekend, no matter what the weather, Denise and Joseph travel out into nature for their spiritual renewal.
   The wilderness is close to their small city where they live. On this day they chose to travel east along the river toward an area below the mountains. It was a warm, spring day and they both felt a sense of peace and contented anticipation as they left the city. They had long ago decided, during this shared ritual, to remain silent during their drive as well as their meditative journey through the nature area they chose to visit. Then, on their drive back into the city, they would then share their experiences with each other.

As they traveled away from the city, they focused their attentions, not just on the road, but also on the fleeting images of bushes, flowers and trees at the edge of the river...and on the river itself. When they drove along this river into the wilderness area, they always felt the currents of the river were flowing into their consciousness — from the opposite direction of their city life state of mind — washing away their normal daily concerns and allowing them to transcend the physical atmosphere from which they were traveling...allowing them to become more open to nature's connection to beyond life dimensions.

Eventually they reached the place where they parked their car and began their ascent into the darkness of the forest...yet into the inner meditative lightness of spiritual dimensions.

As they walked through the forest wilderness, they would notice dying or dead trees and undergrowth, as well as the growing seedlings of young trees and the sprouts of new bushes and vibrant flowers — representing the cycles of death and rebirth. They had long ago recognized nature was expansively connected to primordial, cyclical beginnings and endings. Meditating on the natural processes of death and the subsequent transformations of new beginnings allowed them to feel peaceful of their own transcending end of life...allowed them to feel the spiritual dimensions connected to something more than the physical sensual natural earth realms — wild and yet peaceful.

At times they would remain still along the riverbank. They would focus on the currents again, this time in a meditative state that they were not able to achieve while they were driving away from the city. Sitting side by side with each other, they would breathe deeply, sometimes while holding hands. They would keep their eyes focused on the river currents, and let the music of sounds of the flowing river, the forests, and the wildlife serenade them. They would tune their consciousness to the winds rustling through the trees, the chirping and cawing of birds, and the trilling and buzzing insects — a mixture of harmonious cadences. During these meditations in nature they would often travel somewhere beyond the forest sounds, beyond the sights of the flowing river currents...into spiritual connections to inner dimensions of renewal.

On this day after their meditations, they began the couple-hour walk back to their car. At one point on their way, they began to notice a strong, pungent smell. They looked deeper into the bushes and finally saw the rotting carcass of a deer. They stared at it for a moment. During their past walks they had, on occasion, come across animals that had died. During these times they would pause in their silence to wish the spirit of the dead animal well in its transcending journey.

Today they felt something different. For some reason Joseph felt like burying the deer deeper into the earth. He started to move to do it. He only had a pocket knife and he knew he would also have to use his hands to dig into the earth, and it would take some time. Suddenly he stopped and looked at Denise and motioned that he was ready to continue their journey back to their car and back to their city life.

As they drove back to the city, Denise asked Joseph what had happened as they stood by the carcass of the deer. Joseph explained that he initially felt an urge to bury the dead deer. Yet as he moved toward the carcass to do it, he heard something in his mind say, "There is no need. A natural transcendence of spirit has already occurred, and now let this body dissolve into the earth naturally."

Joseph said he felt a presence surrounding the decaying body of the deer...a presence similar to those he was able to envision during this meditation in which he seems to connect with beyond life dimensions. He said he felt peaceful leaving the process of death and renewal to occur in its natural earth realm time.

Denise said she somehow knew what he had wanted to do, but she also had felt that it was not necessary. For the remainder of their drive home they shared their experiences of communing with nature during their walk and connecting with something more during their meditations as they sat in stillness by the flowing river.

This time during their drive, the river currents were flowing in the direction of their return to their city life, and they both expressed a sense of joy as they imagined they were river rafting back into their daily life activities with a spiritual sense of renewal.

They knew that the experiences of connecting with spiritual dimensions as they meditated in nature also helped them develop the capacity to connect with the same spiritual dimensions at times while engaged in their city life...activities like cooking bread, washing dishes, riding a bus, listening to a concert, fixing something broken in the house, cuddling and making love with each other...and they had often expressed their thanks for helping each other to develop these capacities. They enjoyed living fully in each moment, but they also knew that their fears of dying and death had been transcended by connecting with this natural process of earth realm endings and afterlife new beginnings.

Spiritual Connections Through Singing

D anielle sings and uses her voice expressing songs and chants to open her psyche to receive harmonious inspirations from beyond life dimensions where she knows she will one day go after she leaves this earth...

"Why wait to connect with these spiritual dimensions?" Danielle long ago asked herself, and then answered, "I am not waiting. I will use my singing to enter a trance that will allow me to enter into the same beyond life dimensions I will transition into after I pass from this earth."

Danielle has decided to use the power of her spiritual connections to not just empower her voice, but also her life with the harmony and beauty of the sacred as she sings and allows her consciousness to transcend her rational thoughts, and at times her doubts and fears and resistances, about leaving this wondrous sensuous earth realm.

At times, Danielle will first begin singing tones, some coming from depths beyond her vocal cords and emanating from her psyche.

Sometimes she sings high notes that she imagines connect her to somewhere beyond the stars.

Sometimes she sits still within the sounds of her voice harmonizing with essences that seem to come to sing with her. Often, she begins to dance as she is singing, losing her sense of self in rhythmic movement accompanying her singing.

Sometimes she remembers a sweet light surrounding her, and then she remembers visions of notes spreading out from her being and into spiritual dimensions as her voice blends with the other essences who have come to join in her celebration of transcendental song and dance...

When I Die — I Would Like to Become a Musical Note

I would like to be transformed into any musical note — but maybe the note of C would be best because it's the most used musical note, and it would allow me to be played in an amazing variety of different kinds of music...I'd like that...my soul would appreciate that...

I would like to become a musical note that could be played in blending melodies within spiritual and classical symphonies inspiring peaceful and comforting emotions to everyone who is listening, everyone who has passed from the earth realm and those who have been left behind...classical music with musicians playing different instruments intricately linked to different emotions within each listener's psyche — the violins with exquisite vibrations of fancy, the drums with intensities of passion, clarinets with delicate tones of joy — all expressing the varieties of emotional earthly experiences as well as evoking the visions of spiritual expanses of dimensions within the afterlife.

I would like to become a musical note sung by a blues singer, expressing the struggles of existing without love, without enough food to eat and struggling to exist within the 99% of an unequal income system, along with systemic racial discrimination people with brown skin have had to endure, and as women, gay, LGBTQ and beyond genders have also had to endure.

After I die, I would like to become a musical note played in lively world music, Reggae... Parisian love songs... Gypsy dance songs...exquisite Japanese music combining blends of vocals and instruments such as the lute, flute and a variety of drums...Latin fast moving salsa and intense tango music...Spanish celebratory flamenco music...spiritual and poetic songs from India.

I would like to become a musical note sung by country singers inspiring listeners to cry in their beers for their lost loves, or to nostalgically remember their mamas, or to embrace the expanses of riding their horses in nature and a variety of other life struggles and joys in their everyday lives.

I would like to become a musical note sung by rap singers, as long as their lyrics are not about violence or misogyny...so I can feel what it is like to be bounced from rhyming lyric to lyric like flying wildly, sometimes haphazardly through the air and space.

I would like to become a musical note sung by the amazing variety of pop singers who capture the hearts and desires, joys of love and dancing, dramas of romantic beginnings and endings and inspires listeners to dance...dance wildly without inhibitions, who dance slowly with emotions flowing through their souls.

I would like to become a musical note that would be played in Jazz improvisations reflecting spontaneous mixtures of urban passion as well as discord.

I would like to become a musical note sung by Opera singers conveying emotional and romantic yearnings, translating tragedies into songs of dramatic resolutions, and singing songs that take the listeners into transcendental journeys that connect their souls to spiritual dimensions.

And as I enter into the afterlife as a musical note, I fantasize that I could be played in a jam session with such musicians as Jerry Garcia, Janis Joplin, David Bowie, Amy Winehouse, Leonard Cohen, BB King, Billie Holiday, Whitney Houston, Kurt Cobain, Luciano Pavarotti, Edith Piaf...just to name a few...

If I Could Choose What I Would Like to Explore in the Afterlife, or Be In My Next Life

Would I be a rock star, cavorting around on stage as an uninhibited performer, loving the attention of hundreds and thousands of fans...would it make me feel like a god or could I do that with spiritual wisdom? Hmmm, let me start with trying to learn how to sing...

I might want to be a fish with shiny scales that reflect light even as I dive deeper into the waters and experience the rush of swimming though waves and currents in streams and rivers, and in the stillness of lakes and ponds, and the immense unknown of seas or lakes or oceans...

I might want to be a bird, flying though the clear blue or cloudy skies and maybe even be capable of spreading my inner wings to fly out into the universe...the darkness of space, visiting and exploring sparkling stars, fiery asteroids, and mysterious planets...

I might choose to be who you are...you who have been my lover, you who have been my teacher, my sister or brother, a stranger from another land, another dimension.

I have experienced my loved ones as closely as I could from the boundaries of my individuality, but if I could become you, I would know you in ways I could never know as just myself. I imagine that being who you are while still remaining aware of whom I am or have been would allow both of us to experience the ultimate blend of love. I would never want to be apart from you after I die, so we would just dissolve into each other — even in our present life as we become blended as two separate beings. Blending and then separating again would provide us deeper levels of love...

Oh Happy Music of Death

I'm dancing with the music of the afterlife surrounding me, as if a peace choir is surrounding my bed...and yet I know I am alone in the middle of the night...but I am seeing myself being carried in a casket down the French Quarter of New Orleans with the sounds of clarinets and trombones creating joyful sounds surrounding my soul...

...and then I find myself on the banks of a river near Katmandu, with my body being washed as I am prepared for my cremation on the river...the sitar player is intricately playing a spiritually lively music, surrounding and celebrating my life on this earth...men and women and children dancing and surrounding me, wishing me well on my new journey...

...and then I'm listening to a woman in Paris serenading me with a passionate song as we stand on separate balconies across a courtyard from each other, looking into each other's eyes, and I realize she's the woman I've loved most of my life, the woman who I've lived with and who passed away, and then as the music begins to fade, she begins to disappear, and then...I realize I am also fading away...into her surrounding embrace as we float away together over the Serine River into a symphony of joy, into the afterlife...oh happy music of death...

Music I Want to Listen to as I'm Dying

I have chosen the songs and playlists listed below mostly based on the instrumental and vocal essence of the music, and not always the lyrics. My additional playlists are listed in Appendix III.

I Transcending Playlist:

1. **Everywhere** (*Pink Martini*)
2. **Serenade** (*Pink Martini*)
3. **Our Shangri-La** *(Mark Knopfler and Emmy Lou Harris)*
4. **Sei Viva** (*Priyo*)
5. **Ocean** (*Priyo*)
6. **Spazio** (*Priyo*)
7. **Canzone Latina** (*Priyo*)
8. **Tu Quieres Volver** (*I Muvrini, Sarah Brightman, Le London Symphony Orchestra*)
9. **Terra E Sole** *(Jim Stubblefield)*
10. **Shadow and Light** *(Jim Stubblefield)*
11. **Angel Standing By** *(Jewel)*
12. **Mediterranean Breeze** *(Jim Stubblefield)*
13. **La Soledad** (*Pink Martini*)
14. **Om Namo Narayanaya** (*Pink Martini*)
15. **Surrender** (*Omar Akram*)
16. **Passage into Midnight** (*Omar Akram*)
17. **Because** (*from Beatles Love Album*)
18. **Imagine** (*John Lennon*)
19. **(Just Like) Starting Over** (*John Lennon*)
20. **Silence of Starts** (*Faiborz Lachini*)

21. **Inanna (From "Inanna"** (Armand Amar)
22. **Who Wants To Live Forever** *(Sarah Brightman)*
23. **Time to Say Goodbye** *(Sarah Brightman & Andrea Bocelli)*
24. **Here Comes the Sun / Inner Light** *(from Beatles Love Album)*
25. **Iris** *(Mediterranean Nights)*
26. **Free as a Bird** *(Omar Akram)*
27. **On the Road Again** *(Willie Nelson)*

II Music from the following Albums:

1. **The Lama's Chant** — *Songs of Awakening*
2. **The Joy of Life** — *Karunesh*
3. **Call of the Mystic** — *Karunesh*
4. **Moroccan Spirit** — *Higher Octave Music*
5. **Love** - *Beatles*
6. **All Things Must Pass** — *George Harrison*
7. **Amore** — *Andrea Bocelli*
8. **Duets by** — *Luciano Pavarotti*
9. **Gypsy Lullaby** — *Priyo*
10. **A voce Rivalta** — *I Muvrini*
11. **I Muvrini Et Les 500 Choristes**
12. **Azure** — *Mediterranean Nights*
13. **Arabesque** — *Jane Birkin*
14. **Songs for Tibet** — *The Art of Peace*

If the transcending moment allows, what music would you want to be playing as you pass?

As Long as I Am Here...

I will attempt to use my words to inspire, to gently challenge myself and others to be open to changes in life and attitudes that reflect growth, while still maintaining an inner sense of stability, and sustaining what reflects the uniqueness in each our individualities as we each expand our beings to embrace conscious choices in this reality as well as in unknown and spiritual dimensions.

I will attempt to use my words and actions to encourage myself and others to connect and embrace the diversity of humanity, and what it means to live with love personally, interpersonally and trans-personally.

As long as I am here in the earth realm, I will try to celebrate romance and intimacy in as many ways as I can...

As the Young Man Died in the Ocean

Maurice had just turned 40, and he had always loved to fish and take underwater photographs in the Pacific Ocean off the coast of Oregon as well as in other locations around the world. Maurice had given himself a birthday gift of a day of fishing and invited Phillip, the man he had been seeing for a few months, to come with him.

They had been fishing for an hour or so, and had been enjoying the time together, discussing a variety of things — their work, plans for the future, their challenges, irritations, and then they had fun joking around. They both felt a loving ease with each other.

They had caught a few fish, but Maurice knew it was the fullness of the time together, in an environment in which he always loved, with a partner he had fallen in love with, that was giving him joy.

Maurice was a nature photographer. He had taken many underwater photographs and videos, and at one point during this outing he told Phillip he was going to take a few underwater photos. During the last few months he had been giving Phillip scuba diving lessons, and had hoped Phillip would be able to come with him on his dive. Only at the last moment, Phillip said that he just did not feel prepared, and Maurice said he reluctantly agreed it would not be safe. He assured Phillip there would be other times to go with him as he increased his scuba diving skills.

Maurice was excited about taking some special photographs that he would give his new partner as a gift. Maurice briefly remembered the moment at one of his photography gallery showings a few months ago when he had met Phillip, who had expressed amazement and appreciation of Maurice's underwater photographs. They had instantly felt attracted to each other, and that the beginning of their intimate relationship.

The sea seemed a bit rough, but Maurice knew how to be careful. While he most often tried to dive with a buddy, he actually enjoyed diving alone while taking photographs. He liked getting fully engrossed in what he was seeing and capturing. Maurice put on his sweat suit, and then gathered his scuba diving equipment together. He felt a little unsure about leaving Phillip alone, but he had shown him how to use the radio to call for help if needed, and Phillip was capable of even driving the boat back to the docks if case of an emergency. Before Maurice checked the level of air in his tank, he heard Phillip yell from below deck, as if he were in pain. Maurice jumped up and ran to see what had happened. It turned out Phillip had just stubbed his toe, and he apologized to Maurice profusely for causing him worry. Maurice hugged Phillip and said he was glad nothing serious had happened.

They both walked together back up to the deck, and as Maurice put on his equipment, Phillip came close and gave him a passionate and lengthy kiss. He told Maurice the kiss was the beginning of a delightful night, and that he would be making a sumptuous dinner for them to enjoy when he returned. Phillip said he looked forward to a wonderfully sensual evening. Maurice said he couldn't wait.

Before he jumped into the ocean, Maurice remembered to check the level of air in his tank, which would last about 45 minutes in normal situations, less in some emergency situation if he had to breathe more heavily. He turned to Philip and said, "With all this romance I've feeling, I almost forgot to check the air." And then kissed Phillip again before jumping into the ocean.

Maurice felt excited as he dove below the surface, and after a few minutes of swimming he began taking photographs of light streaming down from the sky above the waves. Then he decided to swim deeper into the ocean to take photographs of what he always enjoyed and referred to as exquisite underwater kaleidoscopic ocean paintings. Actually, the kaleidoscopic affects were created later during his digital editing, but sometimes he envisioned the look of the final photograph while he captured it underwater. Today he wanted to take photographs of the flowing mixtures of light and dark hues and shades at various depths beneath the ocean surface. Maurice was aware that he needed to be careful to not go too deep, but today he felt especially emboldened.

On the deck above him, Phillip was enjoying a beer, but was beginning to feel anxious because he was not used to being in the ocean. He began to worry about the man with whom he had fallen in love. The waves seemed to be getting rougher.

Maurice swam down to about 30 ft. He had always had a streak of spontaneity that bordered on risk-taking, but he felt that he took his best photographs when he knew he was on the edge of safety. As he took photographs on this day, he was amazed at what he was seeing. There was something unusually ethereal about the shades of blue-gray hues.

He decided to go deeper to take advantage of the emotional creativity he was feeling, and did feel something special was about to happen. He realized that his feelings were being stimulated by the joyful development of his love relationship with Phillip. And yet he felt he was also experiencing something else during these moments of underwater inspiration.

The light of his incandescent head lamp allowed him to capture exquisite swirling blends of colorful water movement. He dove deeper. In the past he had swum down to 100 feet briefly, and knew he had to be careful to avoid the effects of nitrogen narcosis.

Suddenly he saw something like a figure moving through the water below him. It didn't seem like a fish or sea mammal. He decided to investigate. He smiled to himself thinking he wasn't that far down to start experiencing hallucinations, but maybe he had seen a merman. Wouldn't that be a kick, he thought, to bring a merman back with him for he and Phillip to enjoy a threesome? He instantly reminded himself that neither he or Phillip was into threesomes, but maybe with a merman they might be more open...

As Maurice dove deeper, he was feeling such an elated sense of discovery. He knew that he was beginning to feel the results of nitrogen narcosis...smiled that he might be "getting narked," yet he still felt he was in control. He giggled to himself as he realized this moment was too special to miss. He felt Phillip would be ecstatic with the photographs he would be giving him. He kept taking photographs as he dove deeper into the ocean's depths.

Maurice became increasingly mesmerized with the sight of swirling waters that seemed to be surrounding him with a caressing beauty. At one point he began seeing or imagining some of the water turning into long hanging curtains of different colors — pearl gray, velvety-looking magenta, and gently undulating amber. These visions reminded him of special moments in his childhood when he visited his grandmother, who hung ceiling to floor curtains in many of her doorways and hallways throughout her house. As a young child, he imagined mysteries existing beyond these curtains — playful creatures, adventurous lands, abundant treats. Now these hallucinations and memories drew him deeper into the ocean as he wanted to explore what was behind these curtains. He continued to take photographs of what he was seeing...imagining what he was seeing.

At some point after these visions, Maurice began to realize he was having difficulty breathing. He did not know how long he had been struggling to breathe. He looked at this watch which indicated he had been beneath the ocean for more than 45 minutes. He was surprised but he still did not feel panicky...instead he felt a joy and comfort as he continued to swim far beneath the surface of the ocean. He remembered the phrase, "Raptures of the Deep" that Jacque Cousteau had described some divers experiencing as they swam deep in the ocean. Maurice had never felt the type of euphoria he was now experiencing, and felt fulfilled in ways he had never experienced before.

It was after that exhilarating thought that Maurice became unconscious...though he did not realize that right away...because he was now outside his body, watching himself sinking deeper and deeper...he saw or imagined himself reaching up and turning off his lamp light...he saw or imagined himself taking off his scuba diving gear...he saw or imagined his body dissolving and turning into a glowing essence of being as it floated toward a white light that had begun to emanate from the darkness of the ocean depths...suddenly he found himself back within his essence of being, the essence of his soul...and Maurice realized his body had not dissolved, but had floated away with the currents of the ocean...while his essence of being continued to float into the embracing light...

As Maurice floated into the afterlife, he hoped that someone would find his camera so that Phillip could see the photographs he had taken for him...but he smiled as he knew that would not really matter in afterlife spiritual terms because he would be able to share the images of his photographs, and so much more, within Phillip's dreams.

When I Die — Remembering My First Breath

I will remember my first breath at the moment of my birth.

The first breath at birth creates and reflects the essence of who we are, who we can be...qualities of being that we can develop in our lifetime in the earth realm...who we are meant to become as a unique individual.

The specific circumstances and outcomes are not predetermined, but are based upon the choices we make in our lives as we develop the qualities that are reflected at our moment of first breath.

As we continue to breathe in and out through the moments of self-actualizing, we can become more aware of our life's potentials through self-study, spiritual attunement, and seeking out caring and wise guidance from others.

Sometimes we lose awareness of our connections to the spiritual dimensions within our psyche, which we can regain in moments of meditation, or other types of spiritual attunement.

As we become older, we begin to appreciate the preciousness of each moment in life. We hopefully can be enriched by the joys of our life, and even if there have been times of struggles, we can appreciate how precious each breath of life has been and will be, even as we will not have to breathe any longer.

First and Last Breaths

The baby's first at birth is synchronistic in reflecting the individual's uniqueness and potentials in life. The first breath you take brings the air of life into your lungs to complete holistic elements of life...Fire (self-assertive and creative energy); Earth (physical body and material resources); Air (rational, synthesizing mind and ability to communicate); Water (sense of emotional well-being and security).

As we grow through life, and as we develop our potentials, we develop and maintain our bodies...we focus our energies hopefully in positive and loving ways...we develop our minds to open ourselves to new ideas, and to communicate with others in respectful and interactive ways...we develop the ability to express our emotions and develop the capacity to feel unconditional acceptance for ourselves, no matter our personal struggles, no matter what our early childhoods have conditioned us to feel...and then we develop the ability to emotionally share with other loved ones in ways caring and transformative...

As we grow through life, and develop our potentials, we continue to breathe — we are guided to take deep healing breaths daily as ways of relaxing, healing, and eventually connecting with higher spiritual dimensions of life.

When we die, our last breath does not end our existence as a unique essence of being.

Your Final Breaths in Your Current Essence of Being in the Earth Realm

I magine that you only have five breaths left before you stop breathing in your current body that encases your essence of being.

As you take your first breath remember how you met the love of your life, your first kiss with the love of your life, the joys of sharing, how you were made to feel special, and how you made your lover feel special...

As you take the second of your five last breaths, remember your family and/or those in your life who have given you their unconditional love, who made you feel loved and appreciated for who you are — remember moments that you would like to take with you as you travel into new dimensions, like photographs of your soul; a series of photographs that you will be able to pull up in your essence of being as you expand through other dimensions...

As you take the third of you last five breaths, bring into your consciousness what accomplishments you have made in your life — accomplishments that reflect your unique and special potentials, and that you are proud of, something you worked for, and something that expresses who you were meant to be in your current life...

As you take the fourth of your five last breaths, think of actions you have done which enhanced the well-being of all life forms remaining on earth, the diversity of populations, the diversity of domestic and wildlife beings, and of earth itself...

As you take your last breath, embrace the warmth of the afterlife — whatever you image the afterlife to be, and if you don't believe in the afterlife...well, hopefully you will be able to embrace the memories of the love, joys, accomplishments and contributions you made in the life you are leaving...and then you will be happily surprised at the expansive spiritual joys you will next be experiencing.

Waiting for My Last Breath

Waiting here in my bed to die from my terminal illness, I wonder when my last breath will fill and then leave my lungs, taking my life force away.

I can feel the other side of life, sometimes I think I can see it — see some of you, who have passed before, who are waiting for me, even visiting me while I am lying here in bed, with my dying body connected to tubes of sorts, catheters, IVs...and with caregivers hovering over me in their loving and sweet ways.

For those of you in this earth realm who are caring for me while I am dying, I am not able to speak, but perhaps I don't need to speak to communicate how much I appreciate the loving care you are giving me, and that when I take my last breath it will be such a joy. And know that I will not really be leaving you. I know that now, and this awareness is allowing me to look forward soon to taking my last breath.

I'm still just aware no matter how much morphine I've been given — I am aware of the essence of my life on earth — my exhilarating, challenging, wonderful life on earth, but I'm ready for the next journey.

Maybe I should be at peace with life and death, and I thought I was, but now that I'm at the transition to my next journey, I'm finding myself a bit impatient to start spiritually travelling.

Yes, I enjoy the presence of my love ones in this earth realm, and I love the smell of the incense. I love the flowers that have been given to me. I listen to the music that calms me. I've always enjoyed many different types of drama, comedy, romance, and travel videos of places I have traveled, and would have loved to travel again if my body was not falling apart.

But I just want to get on with it. Yet I do want my loved ones to know that I know I will remember them, and that I will carry their love and spirits in my soul no matter where I go after I pass. I appreciate their caregiving and love fully in my soul.

Knowing my time has come to transcend, I'm waiting for my last breath with such anticipation...it almost takes my breath away...I wish it would hurry up and do so.

When I Die — Returning to the Womb

I f I choose to reincarnate, I might choose to return to the comfort and full embrace of the womb...we begin to forget...our developing egos begin to forget as we take our first breath after leaving the comfort of the womb. Our developing egos begin to forget our past lives as the sparks of life grow within us.

But those of us who have been able to build the fires of the soul within are able to create emotional and spiritual comfort within ourselves, and only seek to return to the spiritual womb of the universe when we pass from this earth realm.

Yet we might seek to be reborn again in a new mother's womb in some physical realm, in some other lovely dimensions to experience again the sensual caressing comfort and nurturing, and then the growth of our new sparks of life.

When I Die — Crossing Into Afterlife Dimensions

I imagine that when I die my ashes will be placed on round tiles in the shape of a mandala containing the full spectrum of colors symbolizing the holistic blends of yin-yang, cardinal-fixed-mutable, and fire-earth-air-water...multi-faceted ways of being that make up all human characteristics, desires, and imbalances. While living in the earth realm, I have strived towards bringing these varied aspects of life into as much of an imperfectly holistic balance as possible in this earth realm...where we all have opportunities and challenges to develop our unique potentials as we prepare for transitioning further into dimensions while each continuing our own unique spiritual journeys.

Then I imagine that when I die the ashes of my body will be placed in an urn the shape of a dragon with wings that stretch broader than the horizon of day and night, from sunrise to sunset...a spiritual dragon that will become alive and stream my soul away from this earth and into the sky before disappearing and taking my essence into afterlife dimensions.

I imagine that when I die, my essence will stream away from my body that has contained my soul through my present lifetime, and that has allowed me to experience such sensual pleasures and emotional blends with those whom I have loved, and that has allowed me to develop and actualize my unique purposes.

I imagine that when I die, my soul will stream away from this reality into my next phase of existence in other dimensions, containing familiar but unknown joys and challenges, all for the spiritual purposes of allowing me to develop and express even more of the spiritual potentials of my being.

Endings and Beginnings

I t's only a new phase, a new beginning of your being when you transition from your life in the earth realm.

When your time comes to transition, your soul will expand and transform into a spiritual collective of existence in which you are not just one, but all. While living in the earth realm, you also have the opportunity to connect to this spiritual collective of beyond life dimensions, even as you develop the unique expression of your soul in a combination of physical, mental, creative, and interpersonal ways. Yet for many of us, the connection to spiritual dimensions takes consistent effort that reflects a maturity beyond self-oriented urges.

The ending of life on this earth allows each of us to reach new beginnings of awareness and an existence of spiritual being and growth — an awareness and existence that shamans, spiritual healers and practitioners and each of us can envision during our lives in the earth realms, during our daily endings and beginnings, sunsets and sunrises, and fall and spring equinoxes.

While living in the earth realm, as we make our choices of changing a habit, a relationship, a career, our home — maybe not totally ending what we have chosen in these areas of life — but consciously choosing what things to let go of, to allow to be transformed...when we make these choices of conscious change, we have the potential of experiencing transformative new beginnings that will allow us to understand more, as well as experience more of life and spiritual dimensions.

And then when the time comes to actually transition into the afterlife, our unique consciousness, which we have each developed during our lives in the earth realm, will be ready to experience the joys of expansive new spiritual beginnings.

When I Die — I Will Be Thankful

I will be thankful for my life...for everything — the variety of life's wonders, surprises, new beginnings, culminations — the opportunities to heal past traumas...

I will be thankful that as a young adult I was able to experience a variety of learning experiences — in college, and later in my own studies and with wise mentors which gave the opportunities to develop my holistic model and overview of life.

I will be thankful for everyone who has given me their support, love and also who have appropriately challenged me with care — a family member (especially my mother and grandmother), a lover, a friend — all who took time to share.

I will be thankful for the romance I've experienced in my life where I have been able to appreciate the shining qualities of someone I've been fortunate to love, and to experience their appreciation of my interactions and responses...the experience of romance where we each express how much we think the other is beyond special.

I will be thankful that I've experienced intimacies with those I've been romantically in love with and those who are family and friends — these intimate interactions and sharing as one has been transformative for all of us.

I will be thankful for being a part of the evolution of humanity...individuals making the progress to overcome the limits of tribalism, nationalism, extremism, inequalities, racial discrimination... to achieve the potentials of collective caring where all of our diverse beings are embraced and provided equal opportunities for sharing in the wonderful resources of our earth...where our earth and climate is cared for and healed.

I will be thankful, as I take my last breath, for having the fulfilling and dynamic opportunities through my life to breathe in the freshness of new experiences that allowed me to actualize my unique and spiritual potentials.

Transcending Mantras / Chants / Reflections

As I drift into the night of my death transition, I look forward to waking to the dawn of my new essence of being.

I am ready to transcend my body and to float away into other dimensions...into timelessness where I can embrace everything, and everything and everyone will embrace me.

I treasure my life in the earth realm and now am open to new beginnings and treasures I'll experience in the afterlife.

I will exist in new ways with the essence of my being blending with all other essences.

Sometimes I'm afraid of dying but then I tell myself to lighten up...the light will be brighter on the other side of life.

I embrace the transition from living in the sensual earth realms to existing within dimensions that include all ways of being

I am ready to die. I have done the best I could to leave things in a good order — nothing is perfect, except where I am going.

I have been fortunate to have the body I've lived within — and now I am needing to experience more the feeling of my soul and spirit of who I really am.

Let me dissolve into the non-hierarchical god/goddess and wonderful blends of these inspirational essences within me.

I am only human...now! As I transcend, I will become something so much more...untethered from my physical body...yet I know my unique consciousness will exist in the afterlife.

Before I Go

I want to let go of life, of all those loving beings around me with ease...with the ease of knowing all of you will be ok, and that each of you will be able to transform your feelings of loss to a joy for my passing into the wonderment of the afterlife.

I want to let you go with love, and while looking into my children's eyes, my lover's eyes. I want all of you to know that you will not be losing me.

I wish I could convey to all my love ones the feeling of comfort that I am feeling as I drift off consciously into the afterlife.

Do I have regrets? — I'm sure I do, but I can't remember them now, and they would only be fleeting concerns that would dissolve in the warmth of the memories of all the fulfilling interactions I've had with loved ones, and of all the satisfying actions I've taken to develop myself and to love those around me and who have given me so much love.

I wish I could take all of you with me, not in a sense of the actual transition of death I am experiencing, but in a brief journey into the wondrous afterlife, like a spiritual vacation to the beach, to Europe or some magical place you've never been before, but temporarily takes your breath away.

Before I go, I hope you know you will see me again, and that I will be with you from time to time, from dimension to dimension, even as you continue your lives in the earth realm and beyond.

Before I Go #2

Hey, I want to apologize if I made you feel bad somewhere along the way in this book, though I am happy you've made it this far despite maybe sometimes feeling bad (even if you just skipped to the past page to read this...you still made it this far). What I am referring to was my challenge to some of you for maybe trying to hide from the fact that you will be dying, and to not prepare in a positive way for the wonderment of transiting into the afterlife when it's your time.

I'm sure you've had so many other things to think about, to do as you navigate the struggles and joys and the opportunities and challenges during each day of your life. All of these multi-demands in the life realms of our earth life make it so damn hard to see beyond time restraints...the financial demands of paying the rent, paying for medical care and finding some enjoyment in eating out, travel, watching a good show, taking a long walk in nature, playing with our children, connecting with family and friends ...and so much more that makes life worth living...

How can we find the time to look into our inner world and beyond to recognize and view the other dimensions of life that exist beyond our rational mind...these dimensions that filter down into our daily life whether we recognize them or not? As we all know, our culture does not encourage us to open ourselves up to these inner dimensions, and especially to prepare for dying.

As I think of dying, as you've noticed I also like to use the words transition and transformation, because these concepts put the emphasis on life continuing beyond our earth form...

But if you are not ready to prepare — to open yourself up to these spiritual eventualities of dying and transition, transforming into all its transcendental glory, transcendentalism, well I understand. I really do. I hate thinking I'm making you feel anxious or uncomfortable.

Maybe you'd like to be surprised…maybe you just are so engaged and infatuated with the daily streams, joys and stresses and possibilities of daily life…maybe spirituality is rather an unknown path and what does that mean anyway…unless you try to find out, but…

Be at peace, everything will be fine, everything in the afterlife is healing and you'll love it and feel at peace whether you try to prepare for your dying/transition or not.

Live your life to the fullest, and when the time is right you will be embraced and encouraged to flow into your next journey whether you prepare or not. You might be thinking that I've just undermined the purpose of this book, but I believe in the spiritual evolution of all of us…and I admit I'm kind of playing around as I go…Wily Wizard has too much influence on me at times.

Before You Go

P ack your spiritual inner carrying case with care, with wisdom, with preparation, and with a spiritual effort. Live fully in the moment, but know you are only here temporarily...whether you accept it or not you are traveling, and visiting this earth realm, before traveling back to your spiritual home. One definition of "home" is that "it's where you come back to when you are away." You may feel the home you created in the earth realm is your home, but you came from somewhere else, and eventually will be returning back home.

Pack your spiritual inner carrying case — prepare through meditations, through studies — all that will help you transcend your fears and your resistances. I know when you are traveling to some other destinations away from home, especially in this wonderful and sensual earth realm, you will find other places that feel like home and where you might want to remain...but there is a true home that will welcome you when you return, and as you transcend into the afterlife, you will also find that you are able to return to visit your earth home whenever you want, though perhaps while you may want to return to your earth realm home at times, you will love the infinite expansiveness and connections you will experience when you return to your spiritual home.

Pack your inner carrying case with joy and care... transcend your fears of death and dying and prepare for a positive passing into the afterlife when that special moment arrives.

Appendix I

Summary of My Beliefs About Spirituality and the Afterlife

I reject the idea that nothing exists after we die.

I believe we journey into multiple realities, dimensions, and possibilities of being — we experience different sides of ourselves.

I do not believe in the specific political doctrines about spirituality and the afterlife, from various religious viewpoints, Christian, Islam, Hindu — even though some parts of these views may be possible and relate to the spiritual dimensions that I do believe in.

I respect the core beliefs that all of these religions have derived from. I believe that all religions derived from humans connecting with the same multi-dimensional spiritual dimensions, and that as time went on, different tribes and different leaders, mostly men, put their do's and don'ts doctrines onto their efforts to use spiritual dimensions to enhance their own agendas — these doctrines mainly were for the purpose of serving political or egotistical desires. I do respect many of the spiritual rituals, and even myths of these various religions, as pathways to spiritual attainment and connection...

I definitely do not believe in the concepts of heaven and hell.

I believe in the concept of reincarnation, but I believe it is a choice of each essence of being rather than related to some punishment or forced by some higher being who has some pre-ordained idea of what the individual has to do to become more evolved.

I do not believe we may eventually evolve to the point where our souls dissolve back into the universal realm where we lose our individual consciousness or essence.

But I like the concept of our soul/ our essence consciousness existing in different dimensions after we leave this reality.

Whatever you believe — explore it — define it — practice it — embrace it — don't wait. You could be transitioning into life-afterlife dimensions at any time, at any age.

Appendix II

My Challenges With Choosing a Title for This Book

The first title I thought about for this book was **Deathstreams.** Then I, as well as a few reviewers, had concerns about this title.

Before writing about these concerns, I want to write about why I like to use *streams* in some of the titles of my books.

For 50 years I have written journals, and at one point chose to describe some of my entries as **wordstreams.** I chose this term because I realized that much of my journal writings were streams of consciousness entries. I often start my journal writings without a conscious direction in mind, and let the words flow. Then later I would go through my journals and choose specific **wordstreams** to revise. Some became poetry, some became prose poems, some became vignettes, and some became a novel.

While these entries started as flows from my psyche without regard to techniques of the craft of writing, I have always valued the technical aspects of writing. I embraced the necessity of revisions as the next and final steps in the creative process.

The first step for me was always letting loose the creative spirit without judgment or worry about technique. If a writer worries too much about being judged or what the end result might be, I have found that the creative process is often stymied before it begins and progresses to the right completion.

Later in life I realized that the term **wordstreams** described how I have been able to connect with the spiritual world — beyond life dimensions; the afterlife. Writing wordstreams has been a creative visualization and meditative process for me, involving using pen on paper (and sometime using the keyboard) to flow past my ordinary rational consciousness to connect with and be receptive to spiritual dimensions.

Therefore, in my search for a title for this book, it was natural for me to use *streams* as a part of a title. I have written collections of wordstreams that I have titled, *Lovestreams, Spiritstreams* and *Travelstreams.* And, of course, the first book in my potential three-part series, *Afterlife Lovestreams.*

So when I first thought of *Deathstreams* as a title, I thought it was appropriate because I wanted this to focus on encouraging readers to view death as a spiritual transition. I wanted to encourage readers to prepare for dying and death in positive ways that would transform any fears concerns they may have into feelings of well-being that would enhance their daily lives, as well as their eventual process of passing.

However, I had concerns about using the word **death** so strongly in the title, and I began to realize that this concern reflects one aspect of what I am writing about in the book. As one friend told me, "Death in the title would make many people uncomfortable and perhaps would diminish their willingness to read the book."

Susan Astle Paradis, who has been especially helpful in reading this book and providing editing and proofreading assistance, wrote in a text to me:

"About the title to your book...remember when you showed me several ideas you had for the title? Was one of them End-of-Lifestreams? Deathstreams does sound dark outside the context of all of your collected writings. Only, in your book, death isn't a dark thing at all. Your book is enlightening about death. You're shining a light on death's darkness, and showing that it doesn't HAVE to be only a sad or scary thing."

Another friend said that *Deathstreams* seemed too final and maybe the title should convey that it is a transition.

At one point, I was looking through one of my journals written a few years ago at the beginning of my writing *Afterlife Lovestreams* and this book. I came across an entry where I had written the title, *Transcending Streams.* One of the definitions of *Transcending is "to exist beyond the material world."* Another definition: *"To be independent of time and of the universe."*

I then decided to change *Transcending* to *Transcendent* to specifically focus on *"extending beyond the limits of ordinary experience...transcending the universe of material existence."* I thought about *Transcendent* and *Deathstreams: Transcendent Deathstreams.*

But then right before finalizing the manuscript, I began to refocus on the main theme I am trying to convey — of experiencing the spiritual connection of the afterlife while living in the earth realm as a way of transcending one's fear of dying. I decided to title the book, *Afterlife Spirit Streams,* along with the subtitles. I felt this title conveyed the essence of the book in a straightforward manner.

I then decided to write about my process of trying to find a title that reflected my goals in writing this book. As mentioned earlier, I feel that my challenge of including the words *dying* and *death* in the title reflects how this natural and spiritual process of transition causes so much discomfort and grief for many people. Our culture has not embraced positive and supportive understandings and rituals for connecting with beyond life spiritual dimensions while we are living in this earth realm. I do believe that over the past 50 years there have been a growing number of resources, books and healers that have been helping people connect more directly to these spiritual dimensions.

I hope this book will add encouragement and insights to readers in making preparations for their own positive spiritual transcendence we will all be experiencing.

Appendix III

Additional Transcending Playlists

I Omar Akram Playlist

1. **Never Let Go** (from *Free as a Bird*)
2. **Surrender** (from *Free as a Bird*)
3. **Passage of the Heart** (from *Secret Journey*)
4. **Shimmering Star** (from *Secret Journey*)
5. **Caravan** (from *Secret Journey*)
6. **Gypsy Spirit** (from *Secret Journey*)
7. **Whispers in the Moonlight** (from *Secret Journey*)
8. **My Hope is You** (from *Echoes of Love*)
9. **Draw Me Close** (from *Echoes of Love*)
10. **Lovely Day** (from *Echoes of Love*)
11. **Free as a Bird** (from *Free as a Bird*)
12. **Finally Home** (from *Echoes of Love*)

II Gypsy Spirit Playlist

1. **Valse de Melody Live** (*Jane Birkin*)
2. **Comment Te Dire Adiu** (*Jane Birkin*)
3. **She Left Home - Instrumental** (*Jane Birkin*)
4. **Alma** (*I Muvrini*)
5. **The Gates of Istanbul** (*Loreena McKennitt*)
6. **Madanitche** (*Kadda Cherif Hadria*)

7. **Bab Aziz** (*Levon Minassian & J.P. Nergararain*)
8. **Fuir Le Bonheur** (*Jane Birkin*)
9. **Codru** (*Djelem*)
10. **Al Sheraa Al Maksour** (*Omar Kharait*)
11. **El Hilm** (*Omar Kharait*)

III Mediterranean Love Playlist

1. **Assaibene** (*Priyo*)
2. **Sei Viva** (*Priyo*)
3. **Chileno** (*Priyo*)
4. **Canzone Latina** (*Priyo*)
5. **Ocean** (*Priyo*)
6. **Curagiu** (*I Muvrini*)
7. **Spazio** (*Priyo*)
8. **Iris** (*Mediterranean Nights*)
9. **Nostalgia** (*Mediterranean Nights*)
10. **Unrequited Love** (*Mediterranean Nights*)
11. **Echoes of the East** (*Mediterranean Nights*)
12. **Nights on the Mediterranean** (*Mediterranean Nights*)
13. **Cyprus Sunset** (*Mediterranean Nights*)

IV Joys of Love, Life and Beyond Playlist

1. **La Soledad** (*Pink Martini*)
2. **A Te Corsica** (*I Muvrini*)
3. **La Donna Cannone** (*Francesco de Gregori*)
4. **Aspettami** (*Pink Martini*)
5. **Pero Te Extano** (*Andrea Bocelli*)
6. **A Morte Di Filicone** (*I Muvrini*)
7. **Imagine** (*John Lennon*)
8. **Stand by Me** (*John Lennon*)
9. **Love** (*John Lennon*)
10. **Jealous Guy** (*John Lennon*)
11. **Woman** (*John Lennon*)
12. **Tears in Heaven** (*Eric Clapton*)
13. **Layla** (*Eric Clapton*)